The Hymenaean Heresy: Reverse The Charges!

A Response to the Charge that the Full Preterist View of Eschatology is the Revival of an Ancient Heresy.

Don K. Preston D. Div.

© 2014
JaDon Management Inc.
1405 4th Ave. N. W.
#109
Ardmore, OK. 73401
dkpret@cableone.net

ISBN: 978-1-937501-12-9   1-937501-12-4

Logo Design: Joseph Vincent

Cover Design by:
Jeff T. McCormack
The Pendragon: Web & Graphic Design

All book titles by Don K. Preston that are referenced throughout this work can be acquired through many major online book distributors as well as directly through the websites below, where you will also find a wealth of additional materials and resources:

www.eschatology.org
www.bibleprophecy.com
www.donkpreston.com

Acknowledgments

This book is the result of a great deal of interaction with a number of people, some of whom agree with my conclusions and some of whom do not. In the case of those who do not, as scripture says, "Iron sharpens steel." So, my communication and dialog with those who disagree has demanded that I sharpen my arguments and refine my logical presentations.

I want to especially thank some sharp-eyed proofreaders such as Stephen Temple, and my wife, of course. I highly recommend Stephen's book, *Who Was the Mother of Harlots Drunk with the Blood of the Saints*? This is an outstanding book.

Likewise, I want to thank my great friend Jim Wade for his proof reading as well as some helpful editorial suggestions. Jim and his wife Sharon are long time friends and Jim's own studies and insights have often proved stimulating and helpful to me.

My gratitude also goes to Jeff McCormack for his usual fine job not only of proofreading but the cover design.

My special thanks to Douglas Wilkinson and his wife, for their expertise in making sure the electronic form was easy to upload and to use by the readers. I don't have a clue how to do this kind of thing, so their help has been invaluable. Douglas has also written a Kindle book, *Preterist Time Statements*, that is a very valuable study guide.

Preface

When I began my own personal struggles with my traditional view of eschatology, the Hymenaean Heresy charge was one I took very seriously, and had to settle in my mind.

I could not stand the thought of being on the "wrong side" of the truth in regard to the resurrection. Paul undeniably condemned Hymenaeus; this is serious stuff. Being raised as an Amillennialist, I automatically *assumed* that the resurrection occurs at the end of time. It is when the decomposed corpse of every human who has ever died, would be instantly reconstructed, revived and raised out of the ground, as the material cosmos was being burned up, right down to the elements.

The problem was, I had begun to come to grips with the undeniable fact that no matter what my concept of the resurrection was, there are multitudinous statements in both the OT and the New which posited that event *at the end of the Old Covenant age of Israel*, and, more specifically, at the time of the destruction of the Jerusalem temple.

Then, I saw the indisputable– and troubling– fact: the NT writers affirmed that they were living in the time of the end. They said repeatedly the end was near. The time for the fulfillment of God's OT promises to Israel had now arrived; it was the time for the resurrection.

To say this was troubling is a huge understatement. I had to find the answers to the issues of the framework for the resurrection, the imminent NT expectation of the resurrection– and the problem of Hymenaeus.

One of the most challenging moments in my studies was when I asked myself: If the resurrection and the Day of the Lord was what I thought it was, how in the name of reason and logic could *anyone*– including Hymenaeus– convince anyone, the end of time had already happened? Such an idea was then, and is now, ludicrous in the extreme. And yet, Hymenaeus was patently having success convincing churches that the Day of the Lord was already past!

Based on that daunting question, I wrote a small work titled *How Is This Possible?* The first printing sold out quickly. Clearly, others were troubled by the same questions. I have since expanded that material, and am including some– but certainly not all– of it in this work to help the reader see the severity of the problem.

Through my studies in the Old Testament and the definition of the Day of the Lord found there, I soon realized that the only conceivable way Hymenaeus could have convinced anyone the resurrection was past was if he held to the idea that the Day of the Lord is not an earth-burning, time-ending event, but rather, a time when God acted *within history*, to judge a nation, a people, a city. With that Old Testament background to understanding the language of eschatology, my understanding of 2 Timothy 2.17f began to take on a totally different, far more understandable, far more logical, and definitely a more Biblical approach.

The huge majority of Christians today still hold to the literalistic view of the Day of the Lord and the resurrection. (However, change *is* taking place!) Perhaps, you, the reader still hold to that view. Believe me, I fully understand the "shock" of hearing, of even *thinking*, the resurrection is past, the Day of the Lord has happened. I fully understand the "gut reaction" appeal to 2 Timothy 2.17f.

The problem is, most modern readers are simply not tuned into the Hebraic way of thinking. They are not familiar with how the Old Testament defined the Day of the Lord. They do not understand the concepts of shame - v - glory that so permeated the ancient Hebraic world view. Furthermore, neither the Amillennial view of eschatology, nor the Postmillennial view, properly understand the role of Israel in the narrative of the last days and resurrection.

Personally, I well remember the shock and even consternation as it finally dawned on me that Paul and the NT writers said their eschatological hope was *nothing* but the hope of Israel, found in the Old Covenant. This was totally foreign to me, to my church tradition. Yet, it is demonstrably true, and the serious Bible student must come to grips with it.

This book addresses some of these issues. My purpose is to demonstrate that all appeals to the Hymenaeus Heresy, as a charge against the full (true) preterist movement are ill-grounded. In fact, those charges reveal the tragic failure of those making the claims to understand the story of eschatology. Time will tell if this work is successful, but, I can say now that those who have read the earlier *How Is This Possible?* book, have seen the incredible issues at stake. This book goes even deeper than that initial work, so, we pray it will help the reader to understand how superficial and false the charge against the preterist movement is.

Finally, in 2004, Keith Mathison edited a book, *When Shall These Things Be?* (Hereafter WSTTB). That book, with chapters by several prominent Amillennialists and Postmillennialists, presented itself as the definitive refutation of Covenant Eschatology (i.e. preterism). The charge of the Hymenaean Heresy was leveled against the preterist community.

This book will respond to and refute the claims made in that book. Although others have, as cited below, done a fine job of responding to *WSTTB*, I also wanted to add my "two cents worth," albeit a bit belated. When examined in the bright light of "cross-examination" I am convinced the open-minded student will be able to see clearly that Mathison's work has fallen far short of falsifying Covenant Eschatology.

Foreword by William Bell

In the continuing search for truth, there often arises a seemingly insurmountable and daunting cause. In our generation that cause is known as Covenant Eschatology, also known as full preterism, the view that all prophecy was fulfilled in the first century. This movement has required a committed and dedicated warrior to champion it. Don K Preston is one man who has faithfully, consistently and courageously given himself wholly to this cause with a tireless, fervent and tempered zeal of wisdom, knowledge, integrity and compassion for God and men in the cause of truth.

Futurist eschatology in all its shades of Dominionism, Dispensationalism, Amillenialism, Christian Zionism and Partial Preterism, stands opposed to this movement. But, futurism cannot stand before the truth of Covenant Eschatology.

Opponents of Covenant Eschatology commonly appeal to Paul's condemnation of Hymenaeus, who said the resurrection was past, 2000 years ago, as the definitive refutation of preterism (2 Timothy 2:17f). In his latest work, *The Hymenaean Heresy: Reverse the Charges!*, Preston meets that claim head on, and the charge is totally debunked -- to put it *mildly*! In this book Preston decimates the charge of Hymenaean Heresy, forcing it to bow in obeisance as a captive of war to the knowledge of God, having succumbed to both edges of God's sword of the Old and New Testaments Scriptures.

Instead of offering us an abbreviated refutation of the erroneous use of 2 Timothy 2.17-19, in the *Hymenaean Heresy: Reverse the Charges*, in his own unique and characteristic style, Preston dissects and critiques all the major eschatological paradigms in the light of this text. He peels back the veil of camouflage and exposes the shame of futurist errors. He demonstrates beyond refutation that all futurist appeals to the Hymenaean Heresy are actually indictments of those who make the charge. In so doing he lays the charge of heresy squarely in the laps of its suitors. Futurism in all forms is indefensible and this work proves it beyond doubt. This is stunning stuff!

Preston establishes both the Old and the New Testament contextual and prophetic background, time and nature of the resurrection, and posits God's relationship with Israel as his tactical approach to methodically disarm the weakness of futurist arguments and paradigms. Without losing the attention of the reader or sacrificing clarity he sets forth the context of this grossly abused passage with skillful insight and critical analysis. His analysis of Paul's appeal to, and application of, Numbers 16 as the contextual source for his condemnation of Hymenaeus will astound you as it reveals how the commentators have failed to do their job.

Preston has left no stone unturned. The emperor of futurism has no clothes. Futurists are now on the defensive. A decisive and fatal blow is struck and the damages are irrevocable.

Bringing a generation of laborious study, research, documentation, debates, lectures, and writings together, Preston stands with a panoramic perspective of eschatology unparalleled by his opponents and peers. The future of Covenant Eschatology is in good hands and our sons and daughters shall lack no advantage. We highly commend this work as an excellent addition to the growing catalogue of excellent resource tools that will serve generations to come, world without end!

> "But shun profane and idle babblings, for they will increase to more ungodliness. And their message will spread like cancer. Hymenaeus and Philetus are of this sort, who have strayed concerning the truth, saying that the resurrection is already past; and they overthrow the faith of some. Nevertheless the solid foundation of God stands, having this seal: "The Lord knows those who are His," and, "Let everyone who names the name of Christ depart from iniquity" (2 Timothy 2.17f).

These words of Paul, written almost two thousand years ago, serve as the basis for modern attacks on Covenant Eschatology,[1] the view that all prophecy, including the resurrection, has been fulfilled.

The revival and rapid growth of the preterist (fulfilled) view of prophecy has resurrected (pun intended) the charge of "The Hymenaean Heresy." Preacher after preacher, and in article after article, those who espouse the fulfilled view of prophecy are labeled as heretics and false teachers based on the text above. I intend to show in this book that a modern application of Paul's strong words is nothing less than a misuse and perversion of the text.

The modern application of 2 Timothy goes like this:

Hymenaeus and Philetus were destroying the faith of first-century Christians by claiming the resurrection was already past.

Preterists today say the resurrection is already past.

Preterists today are guilty of the same error as Hymenaeus and Philetus.

---

[1] *Covenant Eschatology* is also known as the full preterist view. This school of thought says all prophecies of the end-times, including the Second Coming, judgment and resurrection, were fulfilled at the end of the Old Covenant age of Israel in AD 70. Biblical eschatology is concerned, not with the end of time, (Historical Eschatology), or material creation, but with deliverance from the Old Covenant of sin and death, into the eternal life of the New Covenant of Christ.

Therefore, preterists are guilt of destroying the faith of believers today.

Sounds logical, ominous and dangerous, right? The trouble is, this "argument" is so presuppositional and anachronistic as to be totally misguided and false. But this has not deterred the opponents of Covenant Eschatology from constantly calling preterists the resurrection of the Hymenaean Heresy. That charge can be found everywhere.

On the Internet site <*www.chalcedon.edu/report/97jul/s03.htm*> (link is now inactive) dated February 14, 1999, Andrew Sandlin cites 2 Timothy 2.17f and calls the full preterist view *Hymenaeus Resurrected*. He calls full preterists *heretical preterists*. A *Yahoo* or *Google* search on the Internet, finds numerous sites utilizing 2 Timothy 2.17f to condemn the rapidly growing preterist movement. Strangely, however, there are few sites dedicated to responding directly to the misuse of 2 Timothy 2. This work seeks to correct this situation.

The question is: Is Covenant Eschatology truly a revival of the Hymenaean Heresy, or are those who appeal to this text guilty of a *hermeneutic of anachronism*? Are they guilty of completely ignoring some critical, foundational doctrines in their haste and desire to castigate what they do not even fully understand? Are they guilty of ignoring the correct exegesis of 2 Timothy 2? Are they guilty of completely ignoring the time and framework the Bible sets for the resurrection? We will consider several areas of study to answer this question.

Our study will proceed along these lines:

Point #1. We will ask a very simple, but very important question about the text of 2 Timothy 2: "How Is This Possible?"

Point #2. We will do an exegesis of 2 Timothy 2 to properly understand the issues at stake there and show that those who attempt to use it against the preterist view are mis-using the text. It has been my experience that those who appeal to 2 Timothy have never once examined the prophetic echoes in the text and how important that prophetic background is for properly understanding what Paul says.

Point #3. We will examine what the Bible says about both the time and the nature of the resurrection, to get insight into how Hymenaeus could make his claim. Our study of the time and nature of the resurrection will focus on Daniel 9.24f. This study will prove the resurrection of the dead was to occur at the end of the Old Covenant world of Israel in AD 70.

Point #4. We will examine Daniel 9 and the prediction that seventy weeks were determined... for the resurrection.

Point #5 Resurrection– The Hope of Israel. We will show that the resurrection, no matter what our concept of it might be, was an Old Covenant promise made to Israel after the flesh. Consequently, all applications of 2 Timothy 2 to some proposed "end of the Christian age" event in fulfillment of God's promises to the church (divorced from Israel) are untenable.

Point #6 We will then look at the end of Israel's history in light of Daniel 9 and its relationship to Romans 11.

Point #7 We will examine Romans 11 even deeper and its relationship to the end of Israel's history and the connection to resurrection.

Point #8 We will look at what I call the Hymenaean Hyprocrisy. A look at how those who throw around the "Hymenaean Heresy" label, are the ones guilty of abusing the scripture.

Point #9 We will look at Paul on trial and the Hymenaean Heresy. Didn't Paul say he was a Pharisee, who believed in the resurrection?

We will examine 2 Timothy 2 further and show that the charge of heresy against Covenant Eschatology needs to be rejected. In fact, we will demonstrate that those who attempt to condemn preterists based on 2 Timothy are themselves standing outside Scripture.

I am unaware of another study of the Hymenaean Heresy like this one. My personal experience has been that 2 Timothy 2.17f is just an easy, convenient "proof text" for those who react emotionally to preterism and who are in most cases grossly ignorant of the issues involved.

Properly understood, 2 Timothy 2.17f stands as a powerful indictment of historical Christianity. Most assuredly the appeal to this text to condemn preterists stands as a lamentable example of how the modern church has ignored the role of Israel in eschatology and God's scheme of Redemption.

POINT #1
HOW IS THIS POSSIBLE?

One of the most critical questions about 2 Timothy seems to have completely escaped the notice of the adversaries of Covenant Eschatology. In an earlier work I asked how it would be possible for anyone to believe that the Day of the Lord had already come.[2]

Do you catch the power of the question?

Imagine, you are sitting in church on a given Sunday morning. You believe, and the church you attend teaches, that the Day of the Lord is an earth-burning, cosmos-destroying event, when every human who has ever died and "returned to the dust" will be reconstituted, their bodies restored and resuscitated. On this given Sunday, the preacher gets up and in his sermon declares: "Folks, I have some shocking news. The Lord came yesterday! Time ended, the earth burned up, all the graves are now empty!"

What would you think? I suspect you would look around at your fellow church members to see their shocked– and perhaps amused– reactions. The preacher is surely joking, right? He can't be serious. After all, you can look out the windows and see trees, grass, perhaps ponds. In other words, you can still see the earth. You look down at your watch and it is still ticking.

The preacher lets his message soak in for a moment and then says: "Now, I know you think I am kidding, but I am not! I am telling you, the Day of the Lord occurred yesterday. The earth and the cosmos, right down to the atomic elements, was destroyed in a moment, in the twinkling of an eye and every dead person who has ever lived came out of their graves!"

Needless to say, about this time, you are thinking the preacher has lost his mind! You and the earth are still here. Time is still marching on. The graves are still full. The sun is still in the sky.

Well, consider: in 2 Timothy 2.17f (and 2 Thessalonians 2.2) Paul was dealing with Christians who were saying "the day of the Lord has already

---

[2] Don K. Preston, *How Is This Possible?*, (JaDon Management Inc., 2009).

come" (2 Thessalonians 2.1-2³); "the resurrection is already past" (2 Timothy 2.17f). Just how in the world could any believer believe such a thing?

Bruce was troubled by the significance of this issue and says, "it cannot be supposed that the Thessalonians could have been misled that the events of I Thessalonians (1 Thessalonians 4.13f, DKP) had taken place."[4] Now, if one were expecting a literal, physical fulfillment of those predicted events, Bruce is surely correct. The same is true of the resurrection. If the *resurrection* is a time when the physical body of every person who has ever died is instantaneously reconstructed and raised out of the ground, not to mention the sea, *just how in the name of reason could anyone convince anyone this had already occurred?*

I have posed this question to opponents in several formal public debates as well as in numerous written exchanges. I have yet to receive a substantive, logical, or even reasonable response. One respondent simply wrote in a letter that the question: "Is a whole lot of bother about nothing." Another said the reason Paul did not tell anyone to just go to the grave yards is because the Romans forbad tampering with graves! I can only say that desperate people give desperate answers.

When Paul confronted error, he always met issues head on, and with devastating logic and argumentation, destroyed the very foundation of his opponents. And consider the following.

When the apostles wanted to prove Jesus had risen from the dead, one proof was *the empty tomb* (Lk. 24.3, etc.). Everyone could see it! When

---

[3] While the King James Version renders this as "that the day of the Lord is at hand", this is a totally unjustified translation. As I document in the *How Is This Possible?* book, the KJV stands as one of the few translations with this rendering, and, there is no actual linguistic justification for that translation.

[4] F. F. Bruce, *Word Biblical Commentary, Thessalonians*, Vol. 45, (Dallas, Word Incorporated, 1982)165.

they wanted to prove that someone *had not risen from the dead*, they pointed to a tomb with bones still in it (Acts 2.29). Peter said David's tomb is still with us today! The obvious application here is, if Hymenaeus and Philetus were affirming the past reality of the resurrection as tradition teaches it, Paul could have, would have done what Peter did and what the apostles did– point to grave yard, either full or empty!

If Hymenaeus was teaching the wrong *concept* of the resurrection, how easily Paul could have negated him by showing that he was teaching the wrong kind of resurrection. Paul could have said, "Brethren, the resurrection is a physically observable event. Hymenaeus is teaching that it is a spiritual event. Hymenaeus does not even understand the *nature* of the resurrection." He could have said, like Peter on Pentecost, the bones are still in the graves! *But, he did not do this.* Why? The only logical reason is that Paul and Hymenaeus were essentially on the same page in regard to the *nature* of the resurrection. Hymenaeus just had the chronology wrong. *Paul did not correct the concept of the parousia/resurrection, he corrected the chronology.*

Is it not *abundantly clear* that Hymenaeus was not saying time had ended? He was not saying earth had burned up. He was not saying all of the physically dead had come out of the ground. He was not saying that all the faithful Christians had been taken from the earth. Thus, Knight suggests, "Their teaching apparently related the resurrection only to the inner spiritual life."[5] Beale concurred with this, commenting on the situation at Thessalonica, where some were saying the Day of the Lord had already come: "Apparently in Thessalonica, as elsewhere, false teachers were claiming that Jesus' future advent had already happened in some spiritual manner' either by his coming in the person of the Spirit (perhaps at

---

[5] George W. Knight, *New International Greek Testament Commentary*, (Grand Rapids, Eerdmans, Paternoster, 1992)414. Knight believes Paul taught a future physical bodily resurrection. He fails to see that Paul did not present that concept in refutation of Hymenaeus. Resurrection is more than a simple "inner change." Biblically, resurrection involves Israel corporately, the Hadean realm and the conversion experience (Romans 6, Ephesians 2, etc.). In other words, resurrection, Biblically, is a multi-faceted thing.

Pentecost) or in conjunction with the final (spiritual!) resurrection of the saints."[6]

The problem with these suggestions is, if the resurrection is strictly reference to personal conversion and the "inner spiritual life" how could Paul deny that the Ephesians of the Thessalonians had been converted and experienced that "inner spiritual life"?

To say the resurrection (inner spiritual change) had not taken place would have been to deny their relationship with the Lord! Was Hymenaeus saying the Thessalonians and Ephesians had truly been converted (resurrected through inner spiritual change) but, Paul was denying that? This is a ludicrous suggestion. Very clearly, Knight has himself missed the point, and wrongly identified the identity of the controversy.

The fact that Paul corrected Hymenaeus' *chronology* and not his *concept* of the *nature* of the resurrection is critical to any discussion of 2 Timothy. Instead of addressing the issue in a scholarly, analytical manner, opponents of Covenant Eschatology sometimes arrogantly, like Strimple, say things like, "Hyper-preterists profess to be completely unruffled by the charge that their teaching falls under Paul's condemnation of Hymenaeus and Philetus. Indeed, they seek to turn this problem text into a proof text for their position!"[7] He cites Dan Harden, who posed the question under consideration, and somewhat contemptuously responds that Hymenaeus could have been successful, "In the same way the hyper-preterists have come up with that 'errant belief,' despite the apostle's having taught such a resurrection and the church having confessed her faith in such a resurrection for two thousand years!" (2004, 314). This is really no answer at all.

---

[6] Greg Beale, *The Temple and The Church's Mission, A Biblical Theology of the Dwelling Place of God*, (Downer's Grove, Ill., InterVarsity Press, 2004)270.

[7] Robert Strimple in *When Shall These Things Be? A Reformed Response to Hyper-Preterism,* Editor, Keith Mathison, (Phillipsburg, New Jersey, 2004)313+. And as a matter of fact, 2 Timothy 2 does support– when properly understood -- rather than falsify, Covenant Eschatology.

Strimple has obfuscated and avoided the issue. He simply says Hymenaeus was a false teacher. But we already knew that, didn't we? The question is, why did Paul not address the fundamental issue of the nature of the resurrection and Day of the Lord? Strimple has not proven that Hymenaeus perverted the nature of the resurrection.

Neither Strimple nor Beale offer a syllable of proof to show that Hymenaeus had a resurrection doctrine different from Paul's concept of that event. They have not explained why the only thing Paul addressed was the *timing* of the event, both in Thessalonians and in 2 Timothy 2.

Strimple says Hymenaeus had perverted Paul's doctrine of the resurrection, altering it into something Paul did not teach. But would this not mean Hymenaeus was affirming the past fulfillment of a resurrection different from the resurrection Paul taught? If that were so, why would Paul condemn him for that? After all, Paul was talking about one resurrection and Hymenaeus was talking about another thing. And if, for example, Beale's suggestion concerning the outpouring of the Spirit on Pentecost is what Hymenaeus had in mind how could Paul deny that?

Yet, Strimple says Hymenaeus affirmed the past fulfillment of the resurrection that he, Strimple, teaches. But that can't be true if, as he says, Hymenaeus had altered the doctrine of the resurrection![8] If Hymenaeus taught the past fulfillment of a resurrection different from what Strimple affirms, why would Strimple condemn Hymenaeus? Only if Strimple and Hymenaeus were on the same page as to the nature of the resurrection could Strimple condemn Hymenaeus for saying that resurrection was past.

As just suggested, if Hymenaeus was saying the "inner, spiritual change" of conversion was past, would Paul have condemned him for this? Would Strimple condemn Hymenaeus for that, and deny that believers had been raised to newness of life? If Hymenaeus and Paul were talking about two

---

[8] The claim that Hymenaeus was saying a spiritual resurrection was past is fairly common among the commentators, because most of them, like Bruce, realize how impossible it would have been for Hymenaeus to say the end of the cosmos, and the literal resurrection envisioned by these commentators had already occurred.

different kinds of events, why would Paul condemn Hymenaeus for discussing a subject different from Paul?

Strimple's claim that Paul had taught a literal resurrection in other places is presuppositional. Paul did no such thing. Strimple does not address the question of why Paul did not refer to his earlier teaching on such a literal resurrection. After all, when Peter wrote about the Day of the Lord, he referred to Paul's epistles. Strimple's "answer" to the question of "How Is This Possible?" fails on all accounts. His failure to address the issue substantively, instead of sarcastically is telling. He simply fails to truly answer the question: Given his view of resurrection, *how could anyone believe it had already happened*!

How could *anyone* convince *anyone* that the traditional view of the Day of the Lord -- an earth-burning, time-ending, cosmos-destroying event, when every decomposed body of every dead person in history is raised out of the ground– **had already happened?**
Opponents of Covenant Eschatology claim that is precisely what Hymenaeus was convincing Christians to believe!

And they claim that modern preterists are Hymenaeus "resurrected" -- Teaching the same error.

Such an idea is ludicrous in the extreme!

POINT #2– AN EXEGESIS OF 2 TIMOTHY 2.17F
THE ISSUES INVOLVED

An issue that has seemingly escaped the attention of those who attempt to use 2 Timothy 2 against Covenant Eschatology is verse 19. Paul continues his discussion of the Hymenaean controversy by giving encouragement to those in Ephesus:

"Nevertheless, the foundation of God stands, having this seal: 'The Lord knows those who are His,' and, 'Let every one who names the name of Christ depart from iniquity.'"

The flow of Paul's discussion is that Hymenaeus said the resurrection was past. However, in spite of that claim, the Lord knows who are His, and Paul appeals to Numbers 16 to drive home his point. What did Hymenaeus' claim of a past resurrection have to do with God knowing His true children? What relationship was there between a past resurrection and the question of the identity of the true sons of God?

Knight and others have noted how Paul quotes here from the LXX[9] of Numbers 16 and the rebellion of Korah (1992, 415f). We ask again, what relationship does that rebellion have to the situation in Ephesus? Why did Paul quote Numbers and bring that story to the mind of his readers, when discussing the situation with Hymenaeus? What is the connection?

The issue in Numbers was one of *authority, a question of identity* (Numbers 16.3-5). Was Moses to be the leader of God's people, or would others share in that authority? The issue in Timothy was, "Nevertheless,...The Lord knows who are His" (2 Timothy 2.19). It is a question of *identity*.

As a preliminary point to consider, I suggest Hymenaeus was saying Moses and Torah remained as the "Voice of God," that Jesus may be the Christ, but, Torah and temple still stood as the authority for God's people.

---

[9] The LXX is the Greek translation of the Hebrew Old Testament.

At this juncture, we need to look a little closer at Hymenaeus to see the significance of Paul's assurances in 2 Timothy 2.19.

WHO WAS HYMENAEUS AND FROM WHERE DID HIS TEACHING COME?

Was Hymenaeus a gnostic as proposed by Adam Clark?[10] Lenski says this proposal is fairly common, but claims the gnostic philosophy "does not extend back into Paul's time."[11] There is considerable debate about Lenski's claims. However, we suggest that Hymenaeus and Philetus were *Judaizers*.

The Judaizers accepted Jesus as the Messiah. They accepted the church as the kingdom. They also clung tenaciously to the Old Law, Old Jerusalem and the Old Cultus. They, therefore, believed the promised Messiah and His New World was *inclusive* of the Old.

The Judaizers, e.g. Hymenaeus, insisted that Old Covenant Israel's things continued valid, the Old World *identified* the true people, with the addition of Jesus as Messiah. The Judaizers believed Israel remained the chosen seed and Gentiles had to be incorporated into that Old World. They believed Gentiles could only find their identity as children of God *by inclusion into Old Covenant Israel's world*. Therefore, they demanded that the Gentile converts, "keep the Law of Moses and be circumcised to be saved" (Acts 15.2).

---

[10] Adam Clark, *a Commentary on the New Testament*, Vol. VI, (New York, Abingdon)630.

[11] R. C. H. Lenski, *Interpretation of Colossians, Thessalonians, Timothy, Titus and Philemon*, (Minneapolis, Minnesota, Augsburg, 1937)801. In fact, a growing number of scholars now believe Gnosticism as such did not exist in the first century, but, was a second century phenomenon. Smith claims: "The first historically viable gnostics came from Egypt."... "There is no clear evidence presented as yet that establishes the existence of a pre-Christian or even a first century Gnosticism." Carl Smith, *No Longer Jews,* (Peabody, Mass, 2004), Intro. p. 3. Smith also suggests, provocatively, that Gnosticism arose among Jews disenchanted with the failure of the eschatological promises of YHVH. (p. 18),

Paul, however, knew, "they are not all Israel who are of Israel" (Romans 9.6f). Circumcision is that of the heart and not the flesh (Romans 2.28f). The question had to be settled as to whether the Old World remained as the chosen, or if Jehovah was in the process of creating a new people with a new name (Psalms 102; Isaiah 43; 65.13-19). Who was the True Seed (Galatians 4.22f)?

The Old World could not deliver from death. It was the strength of sin (Romans 7.7f) and the ministration of death (2 Corinthians 3.6f). The Law was weak through the flesh and could never deliver from the law of sin and death (Romans 8.1-4). While it was perfect for the purposes intended, the Law was imperfect to save (Romans 5.21; Galatians 3.20-21; Hebrews 8). For the Judaizers, therefore, to insist that Christ's New World was inclusive of the Old Law was destructive to the salvation by grace Paul taught. The "resurrection," Christ's New World of Life and righteousness, could not be complete while the Old World remained (Hebrews 9.6-10). For Hymenaeus to suggest that the New World was perfected, inclusive of the Old World, therefore, was to say the resurrection was past and overthrow the faith of some by insisting on the continued observance of the Old Law. It was to continue in Law and not go on to Grace and they could never be perfected by the Law (Galatians 3.1-5).

The controversy, therefore, between the Judaizers and Paul was a question of identity, of authority, *just like the story of Korah*. By echoing the story of Korah, and bringing that story into his controversy with Hymenaeus, Paul was following well known Rabbinic "midrash" (commentary) practices. This is often lost on modern readers but was the accepted hermeneutic of Paul's day. This means Paul was telling his audience that the situation in the days of Korah bore strong resemblance, in principle, to that of Hymenaeus. But, just as YHVH settled that controversy, He would settle the Hymenaean controversy.

How was the controversy with Korah settled? We return to Numbers 16, where Paul has taken us.

GOD'S SIGN OF SON-SHIP
In the rebellion of Korah, Jehovah told Moses to inform the people, "Depart now from the tents of these wicked men! Touch nothing of theirs, lest you be consumed in all their tents" (Numbers 16.26). The Lord was to

give a sign that would settle the issue of His chosen. Moses said, "If these men die naturally like all men, or if they are visited by the common fate of all men, then the Lord has not sent me. But, if the Lord creates a new thing, and the earth opens its' mouth and swallows them up with all that belongs to them, and they go alive into the pit, then you will understand that these men have rejected the Lord" (Numbers 16.29f).[12] As Moses said, "The Lord will show who is His, and who is holy" (Numbers 16.5). The Lord would settle the question about the identity of His chosen *by bringing judgment on the rebellious.*

This issue of SON-SHIP is the burning issue in much of the New Testament. We find it as early as the ministry of John the Immerser who castigated the hypocritical Pharisees and Sadducees who came to him, "Who has warned you to flee from the wrath that is about to come? And do not think within yourselves to say, 'We are Abraham's seed' for I say unto you that God is able of these very stones to raise up children unto Abraham" (Matthew 3.7f).

John's statement concerning the seed question, combined with his warning of impending judgment, could only forebode a horrific future for the nation. The "wrath to come" was nothing less than the Great and Terrible Day of the Lord that Elijah, embodied in John, was to proclaim to Israel (Malachi 4.5-6).[13] It is the "wrath to come" that Paul, in Thessalonians, was also anticipating (1 Thessalonians 1.10). This was to be the time when the persecutors of Christ's followers, the true seed of Abraham (Galatians 3-4),

---

[12] It is interesting that God calls the judgment of Israel in AD 70 an "*unusual act*", meaning it would be something they did not expect (Isaiah 28.21). See my *Like Father Like Son, On Clouds of Glory*, for an extensive discussion.

[13] See my 13 Lesson DVD series on Malachi in which I examine the role of John as Elijah and the incredible implications of this for a proper understanding of Biblical eschatology.

would be, "punished with everlasting destruction from the presence of the Lord, and from the glory of His power" (2 Thessalonians 1.9).[14]

Nesbitt stated long ago, "'Destruction from the presence of the Lord, and from the glory of His power' appear to me to have a singular propriety in them, when applied to the ruin of the Jewish nation; for God's presence was the peculiar privilege of that people; which they could only forfeit by their wickedness, and their forsaking the covenant of their God."[15] (See Jeremiah 23.39-40, DKP). In contrast with those to be cast out of the presence of the Lord, Christ's followers, the true seed of Abraham by faith, were to be gathered, identified, vindicated, glorified and relieved from persecution at Christ's coming in fire against their persecutors (2 Thessalonians 1.4f). The issue was one of *identity*.

Notice how Peter drives this home in Acts 3.19f. He called on his audience to repent, so that YHVH would grant them a time of respite prior to the coming judgment. He called their attention to Jesus as the fulfillment of God's promise to Abraham, as well as to Moses and Israel. Notice carefully his words:

"For Moses truly said to the fathers, 'The Lord your God will raise up for you a Prophet like me from your brethren. Him you shall hear in all things, whatever He says to you. And it shall be that every soul who will not hear that Prophet shall be utterly destroyed from among the people" (Acts 3.22-23).

Peter makes it clear that those who would refuse to believe in Jesus as Messiah / Prophet, would not be in obedience to Moses and they would be "cut off" (literally "utterly destroyed," (from *exolethreuthesetai*) "out from among the people" (*ek tou laou*). Notice carefully, those who rejected Jesus are no longer called "the people." The followers of Christ would be "the

---

[14] See my *In Flaming Fire,* for an in-depth discussion of 2 Thessalonians as a statement of the final casting out of the Old Covenant, rebellious seed.

[15] N. Nisbett, *The Prophecy of the Destruction of Jerusalem,* (1787, p. 24). Reprinted by John Bray Ministries, P. O. 90129 Lakeland, Fl. 33804.

people." This is a radical re-definition of "the people" as people of faith, not race. The remnant of Israel, those who accepted Jesus as Messiah, and anyone and everyone that likewise accepted him by faith, would be "the people. But, those of Israel who rejected Him, would no longer be "the people.

In Romans, Paul taught that the Abrahamic seed of the flesh was no longer true Israel[16] (Romans 2.28f; 9.6f). In Galatians 4, his famous allegory is about SON-SHIP; who are the chosen seed of Abraham? Is it the physical seed of Abraham or the spiritual? Paul's declaration is emphatic, "the Jerusalem that now is, and is in bondage with her children" (Galatians 4.25), was Old Covenant Israel according to the flesh and was to be cast out (Galatians 4.30). In Philippians 3.2, Paul addresses the church and says, "We are the circumcision," a contrast and claim against the Judaizers, as well as Israel.

I suggest that the question and controversy about Son-Ship also lies at the heart of Romans 8.18f, where Paul said" creation" longed for "the manifestation of the sons of God." Does not this eager desire to see and experience that identity and manifestation suggest there was controversy and doubt about that issue?[17]

The issue of SON-SHIP and identity is in Revelation also. Jesus assured the churches in Smyrna and Philadelphia that He was aware of their conflict with *the synagogue of Satan* and, "those who say they are Jews, but are not, for they are liars" (Revelation 2.9; 3.9). The Lord assured them He was

---

[16] In truth, those who put their trust in the flesh never had been true Israel! Throughout the OT, the true circumcision was of the heart and humble obedience was the key, not the temple, not the Land, not the sacrifices, but, the heart of faith! See Jeremiah 7 for instance.

[17] Whoever or whatever one identifies as "creation" in Romans 8, it / they were longing to not only *be*, but to be manifested as, "the sons of God." It is almost ludicrous therefore, to suggest that "creation" is to be identified as "bugs, slugs and mosquitoes!" Are bugs truly longing to be identified as Sons of God?

about to come and, "I will make them come and worship before your feet, and to know that I have loved you" (3.9). The fall of *Babylon*, the city "where the Lord was slain" would be the ultimate sign of the identity of God's true people.[18] The Lord would bring judgment on those claiming to be the Sons of God, but who were in fact, rebellious against God's chosen.[19]

Franklin Camp noted, "The fall of Jerusalem settled the question as to who are the sons of God. The struggle between the Jews, Judaizing teachers, and the apostles, especially the apostle Paul, runs through all the epistles."[20] The truth of this statement can hardly be denied, and there can be no doubt that in 2 Timothy 2.17-19, one of the issues is the identity of the Sons of God, for Paul takes note of Hymenaeus and then says *"Nevertheless*, God knows who are His" (my emp.). Paul was saying that in spite of Hymenaeus' claims, God knows His (true) children.

Thus, Paul's use of Numbers contains the implicit, but clear warning of impending judgment on the "false children." Just as God gave Israel a sign -- the destruction of Korah and his followers -- that identified the true Sons of God, He was about to give another sign to confirm the identity of the True Israel. He would destroy the Old World, thus removing any argument of the Judaizers, Hymenaeus and his followers, not to mention the Jews, for

---

[18] This idea is developed even more in my book *Who Is This Babylon?*. The fall of Babylon would make manifest the children of God. Only the fall of Jerusalem would settle the on-going and severe conflict over this question. The fall of Rome, Roman Catholicism, America, the Common Market, etc. is totally unrelated to controversy over SON-SHIP.

[19] I personally see Revelation 2-3 and the raging controversy about the identity of the true "Jew" and the promise of the imminent divine answer to that question, as a definitive commentary on Romans 8.

[20] Franklin Camp, *The Work of the Holy Spirit in Redemption*, (Birmingham, Ala., Roberts and Sons Publications, 1974)55.

saying the Old World remained the focus of God's attention.[21] The Judaizer's argument that God had completed His work, that the resurrection had been perfected *and included the Old World*, would be definitively shown to be false.

---

[21] It is worthy of note that Paul had delivered Hymenaeus to Satan (1 Timothy 1.20). McClintock and Strong, *Encyclopedia of Biblical, Theological, and Ecclesiastical Literature*, Vol. IV, (Grand Rapids, Baker, 1969)431f, effectively show that this means more than *excommunication*, it involved *punishment*. (Compare Acts 5, 1 Corinthians 5.5; 1 Corinthians 11.29f). So, if those who are making the charge of the Hymenaean Heresy today, are correct, perhaps they should demonstrate the same divine power manifested by Paul in delivering Hymenaeus to the Devil.

Point #3
THE TIME AND NATURE OF THE RESURRECTION

I want to ask again how would it be possible for Hymenaeus to teach what he did? He surely thought he had support for his views. Was not Jesus the first fruits from the dead? If the first fruits had come, had not the harvest time arrived? Did not Paul himself, proclaim that resurrection from the dead was a present reality (Romans 6.3-5, 9-11; Ephesians 2.1-5; Philippians 3.9-16; Colossians 2.12-13; 3.1f)? Had Paul himself not told the Romans, "reckon yourselves to be alive from the dead" (Romans 6.11)? Had he not told the Colossians they had *risen* with Christ, from the dead? Hymenaeus, therefore, *ostensibly*, had somewhat of a case, for as King well stated, "The question is not whether the eschatological resurrection had begun, but whether it was a completed or consummated work of the quickening Spirit?"[22]

Did Hymenaeus have grounds for saying the *time* for the resurrection had come? Indeed. He knew Jesus had come at *the end of the age* (Galatians 4.4; Hebrews 1.1; Hebrews 9.26) and the resurrection was to occur at the time of the end (Daniel 12.2-4; Matthew 13.39-43). Thus, the time for the resurrection was present. He could hardly have been unaware that even Paul said, "the end of the ages has come upon us" (1 Corinthians 10.11). Was he not also aware that Peter said Jesus was, "ready (Greek, *hetoimos*[23]) to judge the living and the dead" (1 Peter 4.5), and, "the time has come for the judgment to begin at the house of God" (1 Peter 4.17)? Thus, Jesus and his apostles plainly taught that the time for the resurrection was present.

In addition, Daniel predicted that the end time resurrection was associated with *the judgment of Israel* (Daniel 12.2-7). Scripture is clear that Israel's

---

[22] Max R. King, *The Cross and The Parousia, Two Dimensions of One Age Changing Eschaton*, (Warren, Ohio, Research and Writing Ministry, Parkman Rd. Church of Christ, 1987)172.

[23] Robertson Nicoll, *The Expositor's Greek Testament*, Vol. V., (Grand Rapids, Eerdman's, 1970)71, says of *hetoimos*, "the Greek readers would understand the *imminent judge*."

salvation, i.e. her resurrection, would come through *judgment* (Isaiah 4.4; Joel 2-3; Zechariah 12-14).

In Isaiah 24-25, Jehovah promised that at the time of the judgment of the "city of confusion" (24.10), for breaking "the everlasting covenant" (24.5), He would "swallow up death forever" (25.8). Thus, resurrection and the judgment of Israel are inextricably linked in prophecy. Hymenaeus even had a Jerusalem catastrophe to substantiate his claim that, if resurrection was associated with judgment on Jerusalem, then it had, in fact, occurred.

There were *two* specific events that had happened in Jerusalem. These might have been used to convince the Thessalonians and Ephesians the Day of the Lord had already come. Either of these events, or both combined, could have been the basis of the claims of Hymenaeus. The incident involving Caligula's statue could have been understood as fulfillment of Paul's teaching about the son of perdition (II Thessalonians 2.5)[24] and the catastrophe involving 30,000 deaths in the Jerusalem temple could have been understood as Christ's wrath on the temple.[25] Thus, the time was right and events in Jerusalem suggested that the time had actually come. But, there was more.

Hymenaeus had even more evidence. The resurrection is inseparably linked with *the establishment of the kingdom*. This fact is sadly ignored or denied by the Amillennialist. Yet, Scripture is plain: death would be destroyed when Jehovah established His rule – the kingdom -- in Zion (Isaiah 24-25).

John saw the vision of the resurrection as the time when, "the kingdoms of this world have become the kingdoms of our Lord and of His Christ" (Revelation 11.15). Daniel saw the time when the books were opened as the time when the Son of Man *received the kingdom* (Daniel 7.9-14). John saw

---

[24] Between 39-41 AD, Caligula commanded that his statue be erected in the temple at Jerusalem. This incident brought the nation to the brink of war.

[25] Josephus tells us that under the Procurator Cumanus, circa 48-52 AD, there was a riot in the temple area of Jerusalem in which over 30,000 people were trampled to death in one day. (Josephus, *Wars*, Bk. II: chap. 12:1).

the time of the opening of the books as the time of the *resurrection* (Revelation 20.12f).[26] Paul said Christ was about to (*mello*), "judge the living and the dead at His appearing and kingdom" (2 Timothy 4.1), and the judgment of the nations is depicted as the time when the Son would "sit on the throne of His glory" (Matthew 25.31f). Thus, the kingdom and resurrection are Siamese twins. They cannot be separated.

When Jesus came proclaiming, "The kingdom of heaven is at hand" (Mark 1.15) this was nothing less than a declaration that the time for the resurrection had come. This is confirmed in the Immerser's message. He proclaimed the imminence of the kingdom (Matthew 3.2) and said the instruments of the *harvest* were already in Jesus' hand (Matthew 3.10f).[27] *The harvest is the time of the resurrection (Matthew 13.36-40)*. If the time of the harvest is the time of the resurrection, and if the instruments of the harvest were already in Jesus' hand, it is undeniable that the resurrection was at hand.

If Hymenaeus knew this, and how could he not, he also knew Christ himself said the resurrection would occur in that generation. This is highly significant.

Gentry, like most futurists, insists that Jesus posited his "final" coming in the distant future from the first century generation. He denies a first century imminence of the resurrection. Commenting on Matthew 25, he claims:

---

[26] In my *Who Is This Babylon?* I show that the judgment at the opening of the books could not extend beyond the days of the Roman empire. The traditional Amillennial posit is that Daniel 7.13-14 was fulfilled in Christ's ascension (Acts 1) and coronation on Pentecost. If this is true, the opening of the books in judgment of the persecuting "little horn" (Daniel 7.8f) occurred at Pentecost. The Amillennial view is fatally flawed.

[27] Note how John said the "winnowing fork" was already in Jesus' hand. What is often overlooked is that the winnowing fork was the instrument to be used at the end of the harvest, after the wheat and tares had been gathered and put on the threshing flood. This magnifies the genuine imminence of the text.

"His return has not been imminent since the ascension"; "The New Testament teaches, however, that the Lord's glorious, bodily return will be in the *distant* and *unknowable* future. It has not been *imminent* and will not be *datable*. Theologically 'distinctive to (Postmillennnialism) is the *denial* of the imminent physical return' of Christ." – "Jesus clearly taught: 'While the bridegroom was delayed, they all slumbered and slept" (Matthew 25.5). "For the kingdom of heaven is like a man traveling to a far country, who called his own servants and delivered his goods to them... After a long time, the Lord of those servants came and settled accounts with them" (Matthew 25.14, 19). There is no expectation here of an any-moment return– there is quite the opposite." (1992, 332). This is really quite bad.

Gentry takes it for granted, while offering not a syllable of proof, that the "long time" of Matthew 25 must refer to the 2000 years since Jesus spoke the parable. This is purely presuppositional.

Gentry's claim that the parousia was not near in the first century is false, as even a cursory look at the NT will quickly show.[28] Imminence of the parousia permeates the entire corpus of the epistles.

Although I don't think he intended to be doing so, Leithart has given a good response to Gentry's claims. Commenting on the scoffers in 2 Peter 3,[29] who said "Where is the promise of his coming," Leithart says, "Even if the false teachers were destroyed, they would eventually be proven right. Indefinite delay of the parousia would be a feeble response to false teachers

---

[28] See my *Can God Tell Time?* for a thorough examination of the objective nature of the multitudinous statements of imminence in the NT. In addition, see Douglas Wilkinson's *New Testament Time Statements,* on Kindle. Wilkinson has documented 250 statements of imminence in the NT and categorized them in an impressive and convincing manner.

[29] Don't forget the question: *How Is This Possible?* How could anyone– applying the language of 2 Peter 3 literally, of a future destruction of the material cosmos -- believe it had already happened? And how could they convince anyone it already happened?

who are predicting that the parousia will be delayed indefinitely." [30] In other words, if the Day of the Lord was supposed to be far off, the scoffers had no argument and Peter could have said so. Apply that to Gentry's take on Matthew 25.

Gentry says Jesus taught that his "real" coming was to be– is– in the far distant future. But the scoffers in 2 Peter 3 were denying the imminence of that coming. As Leithart notes, if Jesus had actually posited his parousia for so far in the future, the scoffers would be making a valid case.

The scoffers were not saying the Day of the Lord was not a *reality*. The OT established the reality of that event. But, they were saying "Where is it?" Their objection, as Leithart correctly observes, was only valid if that predicted Day was supposed to have been imminent in their day.

So, per Gentry, Matthew 25 posited the parousia for the distant future, thus nullifying any objection by the scoffers that it had not occurred. Gentry says 2 Peter 3 speaks of the same Day of the Lord as Matthew 25. But the objection of the scoffers in 2 Peter 3 would only be valid if the Day of the Lord was supposed to be imminent enough for them to say "Where is it?" So, either Gentry is wrong about the parousia in Matthew 25 or 2 Peter 3 is speaking of a different coming of the Lord from that in Matthew 25– which Gentry rejects.

If, as Gentry and other Dominionists say, Jesus spoke of an indefinite but objectively long time before the parousia / resurrection, this would have immediately and definitively falsified Hymenaeus. If Jesus and the NT writers all said the parousia and resurrection was to be a far distant event removed in time for perhaps millennia from the first century, would it not have been down right silly for Hymenaeus to say it had already happened? Would not someone, perhaps even Paul, have said: "Look, Hymen, we all know Jesus said his coming and the resurrection would not be for a long, long time. It is crazy for you to say it has already happened, since it has only been a few years since Jesus ascended."

---

[30] Peter Leithart, *The Promise of His Coming*, (Moscow, Idaho, Canon Press, 2004)67.

Further, since the kingdom and resurrection are inseparably linked, we must reiterate the fact established elsewhere in this work that resurrection is also associated with the judgment on Israel (Isaiah 24-29; Daniel 12). *This is significant because Jesus associated the fall of Jerusalem with the kingdom and His parousia in Luke 21.*

In His prediction of Israel's judgment, Jesus said in that event the kingdom would be at hand (Luke 21.31f).

In scripture then, resurrection, kingdom and the judgment of Israel are all inseparably linked. If Hymenaeus knew all of this, then linked with the events we have noted above, Hymenaeus *seemed* to have a powerful argument.

If the kingdom and the resurrection are related, what then is the *nature* of the resurrection? Is it discernible with the human eye? Why did Paul not tell Hymenaeus and the Ephesians, "My eyes are not seeing what my ears are hearing, Hymenaeus!"? Why did Paul not tell his readers to go to the cemetery and open their eyes? Because the resurrection is associated with the kingdom, *it is not a visibly discernible event.*

The Pharisees approached Jesus and asked when the kingdom of God would come (Luke 17.20). Jesus' response is critical, "The kingdom of God does not come with observation." If the kingdom and the resurrection are inseparably linked, and if the kingdom is *not with observation*, why is the resurrection a visible event?[31]

When Paul discussed the resurrection change from the outward man that was perishing to the inner man "not made with hands, eternal in the heavens" in 2 Corinthians 4-5, he said, "we do not look on the things that are seen, but at the things that are unseen" (2 Corinthians 4.16f). This is an

---

[31] This is part of the self-contradictory nature of Dominionism / Postmillennialism. On the one hand, when debating Dispensationalists, they affirm the spiritual, unseen nature of the kingdom. However, in my July 2012 formal debate with Joel McDurmon, he said we are waiting for the establishment of a physical, earthly kingdom. That debate book: *End Times Dilemma* is available from my websites.

emphatic declaration that the resurrection was not a visibly discernible event. We will have more to say on this below, when we discuss Paul and his trial when the Pharisees sought his life for his views on the resurrection.

For the moment however, consider a text from 2 Timothy 2, the very text in which Paul condemned Hymenaeus. Paul has something to say here about resurrection that is often overlooked in regard to the Hymenaean issue. Take a look at 2 Timothy 2.11-12:

> "This is a faithful saying: For if we died with Him, We shall also live with Him. If we endure, We shall also reign with Him. If we deny Him, He also will deny us."[32]

This text is highly suggestive. Paul said the Ephesians had died with Christ (*sunapethanomen*, aorist– past tense). I think we are on safe ground in saying they had not died physically! While they had died– and thus, in Pauline theology, they were, when he wrote, in that state of "death"– nonetheless, he expressed the full confidence "we shall live with him."

Is it not axiomatic that the resurrection life Paul was anticipating would bring to an end the "death" they were currently under?[33] (It might be more

---

[32] It is unfortunate how some commentators seek to mitigate the past tense nature of the death here, and posit it as future, to speak of the possible martyrdom of Timothy and his audience. Mounce cites Lock who renders this verse as, "Who shares Christ's death His life shall share." (William Mounce, *Word Biblical Commentary, Pastoral Epistles,* Vol. 46, (Nashville, Nelson Publishers 2000)515). But, this is a clear violation of the text. It is neither the subjunctive nor the future. It undeniably speaks of a past "death" that had already been experienced by the Ephesians believers.

[33] Note the parallel with Romans 8.10– "And if Christ is in you, the body is dead because of sin, but the Spirit is life because of righteousness." Again, it is patently obvious Paul was not talking about their physical body being dead because of Christ dwelling in them! (That would mean that to enter the death of Christ would be to come under the curse of another death, in addition to the Curse of Adam!) And, it is equally

technically accurate to say they had died with Christ, and their life in Christ was *hidden*, Colossians 3.1-3, to be *manifested* at the parousia. However, the end result is the same. The future life was clearly not physical life, for it would match in nature the "death" they had died). They would be delivered from that death to life. If the death they were experiencing was not biological death, it is undeniable that it would not be physical resurrection that would be the removal of that death.

So, Paul is here affirming a non-biological, non-physical resurrection that was future to him. And it is in *that* context he then immediately condemned Hymenaeus for saying "the resurrection is past already." What resurrection had Paul mentioned? It was the non-literal, non, physical, non-fleshly resurrection. It was the resurrection to spiritual life. Does Paul suddenly, with no indication at all, shift discussion to another, radically different resurrection?

Unless one can demonstrate that in 2 Timothy 2.17f, Paul introduces a different death and resurrection doctrine from that which he discusses in verse 11, this serves as powerful evidence that Hymenaeus was not affirming the past occurrence of a physical resurrection of corpses. He was affirming that the redemptive story was over, consummated, but as we have seen, this would mean Torah and temple remained as God's authoritative Law and Locus, and Paul would have none of that.

It should be more than obvious that the resurrection of verse 11 and the resurrection controversy with Hymenaeus in v. 17f is the same resurrection. It is revealing and significant therefore, that *none* of the authors in *WSTTB*, so much as mention the connection between verse 11 and verses 17f. This is a critical and fatal oversight, and suggests they simply desired to proof text, and "cherry pick," Paul's condemnation of Hymenaeus instead of actually engaging in serious exegesis of the text.

---

clear that this "death" they were under was not a curse, but a death they had to die in order to live! See also Romans 6 where Paul had earlier spoken of the Romans entering the death of Christ and were looking forward to life in him. Once again the "death, looking toward life" motif simply cannot be referent to biological death and life.

There is no excuse for ignoring Paul's earlier discussion of death and resurrection, which patently is not a discussion of the raising of human corpses, and then imposing a radically different concept of death and resurrection onto verses 17f. How in the name of reason– and scholarship -- can you totally ignore Paul's discussion of death and life in the context, and then just point to verse 17f claiming it is a discussion of something foreign to the context?

So, here is what we are saying about the context of 2 Timothy 2.17f:
✢ In 2 Timothy 2.11 Paul discusses death and life (resurrection).
✢ *He says the Ephesians had already experienced "death."*
✢ The resurrection he was anticipating would be the end of that "death."
✢ But, the Ephesians had clearly not died physically!
✢Therefore, the resurrection Paul was anticipating was not the raising of human corpses.

This is the context of the discussion of Hymenaeus' error on the resurrection, and demonstrates that the controversy was not about the raising of human corpses out of the ground!

Hymenaeus was affirming the past reality of the resurrection– non-biological resurrection– Paul was still looking forward to it.

Only by doing violence to the text can one get physical resurrection out of Paul's discussion.

WHAT, THEN, ABOUT "EVERY EYE SHALL SEE HIM"?

It is often rejoined that John says, "every eye shall see Him" (Revelation 1.7), and therefore, Jesus' *parousia*, the establishment of the kingdom and the resurrection must be visible events. Interestingly, even many of those who oppose Covenant Eschatology recognize that this is an invalid argument.

(Again, don't forget the question: *How Is This Possible?* If the coming of the Lord is an event seen by every human that has ever lived and every human alive on the planet at that moment, how could anyone believe it was already past?)

Stafford North, in a lecture delivered in 1990, commented on Matthew 24.30, "Whenever Christ is said to move on the clouds, the reference is not to a physical coming, but to a spiritual one. Just as God came on the clouds to destroy Egypt (Isaiah 19), so Jesus came on the clouds to destroy Jerusalem."[34] North posits Revelation 1.7 as a prediction of Christ's coming against Rome. Nevertheless, he understands the language of Revelation 1.7 cannot be interpreted literally.[35] It is typical apocalyptic language to describe God's actions in judgment.[36]

Significantly, many of those who insist on the visible, physical *parousia* and resurrection are vehement in recognizing the apocalyptic language of Matthew 24.29-31.[37] Those who often do a fine job of showing the metaphoric nature of the language of Matthew would do well to apply their own understanding of apocalyptic language to Revelation 1.7 and *see*

---

[34] Stafford North, Oklahoma Christian University of Science and Art, Edmond, Ok., Annual Lectureship, 1990, *Did Jesus Return in AD 70?* I was present at that lecture and sat amazed at the inconsistency of North's comments. At the end of his presentation, I challenged him to a public debate on the issue. He informed me he did not know enough about the issue to debate it.

[35] It seemed to have escaped North's attention that 1 Thessalonians 4.13f is a coming of Christ on the clouds. If Christ's cloud comings cannot be interpreted literally as North suggests, how does he justify his literalistic interpretation of Thessalonians? See my *We Shall Meet Him in the Air, The Wedding of the King of kings,* for an in-depth discussion of this kind of language.

[36] We recommend John Bray's, *Matthew 24 Fulfilled*, (John Bray Ministry, P. O. Box 90129 Lakeland, Fl. 33804); and Gary DeMar's, *Last Days Madness: Obsession of the Modern Church*, (American Vision, Atlanta, Ga.) as two good sources explaining the apocalyptic language of scripture.

[37] See for instance Lorraine Boettner, *The Millennium,* (Philadelphia, Presbyterian and Reformed Press, 1957)252+; Marcellus Kik, *Eschatology of Victory*, (Philadelphia, Presbyterian and Reformed Press, 1971)127+.

(*small* pun intended) the inconsistency of their interpretation. If they can *see* that the *parousia* of Matthew 24 was to be *seen*, but was not an optical event, they can surely *see* that the resurrection could also not be an optical event.

It should be observed that John, in Revelation 1.7 provides a definite hermeneutical key to understanding the framework and nature of the *parousia* and thus the resurrection under consideration. In the very text that speaks of "every eye" seeing Him, it identifies who was to be the focus of His coming. It was to be "Even those who pierced Him."

This is nothing less than a statement that the coming of the Lord in Revelation was to be against those who crucified Him! Who was that? In Revelation 11.7, we are told the judgment of the Great City was the judgment of the city "where the Lord was slain"; this can be no other city than first century Jerusalem. Revelation is the unfolding story of heaven's response to the prayer of the Jews "Let his blood be on us and on our children!" (Matthew 27.25).

In other words, Revelation is typical prophetic and apocalyptic language to describe God's actions against His enemies. The language is highly metaphoric and figurative, being taken directly from the Old Testament prophetic scriptures that described the Day of the Lord as anytime God acted in history. Just as God "came" on the clouds of heaven in the Old Covenant era to judge Egypt, Assyria, Babylon, etc., He was going to come against the city that had slain His Son. Those who pierced Him would mourn as He rode on the clouds in judgment against them.

Interestingly, in *WSTTB*, Kistemaker (p. 253) insists that Revelation 1.7 speaks of a yet future, end of time coming of Christ when every human on the globe sees him coming. This puts him at severe odds with Gentry and Mathison both. Mathison cites Gentry, with approval, and Gentry applies Revelation 1.7 to the coming of Christ in AD 70 (Mathison, 1999, 143)! Thus, the glaring inconsistency and self-contradiction of the contributing authors to *WSTTB*, is revealed. Mathison's inclusion of Kistemaker, knowing full well that Kistemaker's view is diametrically opposite and opposed to his own view, gives the impression that Mathison was essentially saying "Any view is 'okay' as long as it is not the true preterist view!"

There is another hermeneutical key here, one emphasized by Jerry Johnson of the NiceneCouncil group, in a helpful and informative DVD.[38] Johnson, commenting on the proper hermeneutic for understanding the Olivet Discourse, says, "Unless a text says otherwise, explicitly or by good and necessary consequence, the intent of any statement must have primary application to the original audience to which it was given or spoken." This is well stated, but of course, it is fatal to his futurism.

There are no texts that posit the resurrection of the dead into our future. Paul, in 1 Thessalonians 4 and 1 Corinthians 15 spoke of "we who are alive" (twice), and "we shall not all sleep." He was writing to his contemporaries, about the impending parousia and resurrection. Does the hermeneutical rule posited by Johnson not apply here? Why not? Where does Paul indicate the resurrection was not for his generation? Where does Jesus ever posit the end of the age beyond the fall of Jerusalem? So, while Johnson's hermeneutic is sound, valid and true, it destroys his futurism, and, it forces us to take a fresh look at the Hymenaean Heresy.

As we have seen, scripture places the resurrection in the context of the judgment on Israel and Hymenaeus could not have been totally ignorant of this. Had he not heard either the apostles say the end was near, or heard that read in the assembly somewhere? He could hardly have been ignorant of the two horrific incidents in Jerusalem noted above. Revelation 1.7, therefore, is no valid objection against the idea of Christ's *parousia* occurring in the first century.

Thus, for Hymenaeus, the words of Jesus, the testimony of Paul, the resurrection of Jesus, the arrival of the prophesied time and historical events all seemed to suggest the resurrection had indeed occurred. The resurrection did involve judgment on Israel, but what happened in 39-49 AD did not qualify as the destruction required by Daniel 12. The resurrection *was* "spiritual," as our discussion above has demonstrated and,

---

[38] Jerry Johnson, "A.D. 70 The Destruction of Jerusalem" (2011). The DVD can be purchased from American Vision, or www.NiceneCouncil.com. The DVD contains some excellent historical and scriptural documentation for the first century fulfillment of the Great Tribulation.

there was a futuristic element being ignored by Hymenaeus (Romans 6.5, 8; Colossians 3.2-4; 2 Timothy 2.11). The resurrection did involve Old Covenant Israel, *but it meant the dissolution of that old shadow world, not the inclusion into Christ's New World. It meant the putting off of the old **body** and the taking of the new **body** in Christ.* Hymenaeus had his timing off and believed Christ's New Order included the Old World.

This brings us back to the issue of resurrection being the hope of Israel. Like those in Thessalonica and Rome, Hymenaeus was saying the Day of the Lord had come, having now fulfilled His Word.[39]

Further, Jesus was the first fruit of the resurrection (1 Corinthians 15.20f).[40] Who then were the *first fruits* making up the *continuation* of that harvest/resurrection? Hymenaeus taught that the resurrection was over, completed, and what Christ had initiated had *now been consummated*. Well, if physical resurrection is the focus, *where were the rest of the physically dead that had been resurrected in immortal, incorruptible bodies?*

---

[39] It *may be* that there is a *slight* nuance of difference between Romans 11 (1 Corinthians 15. 12f also), where some were saying that Israel had been cut off and Thessalonians and 2 Timothy 2 where it was being said that Israel's eschaton, the Day of the Lord and Resurrection, had already come. It may be, although I am not totally convinced, that those in Rome wanted to say that God had cut of Israel *without fulfilling His promises to her*. This Paul emphatically denied (Romans 11.1-7, 25f). This is certainly not the issue in Thessalonians and Timothy. To affirm the reality of the Day of the Lord and Resurrection was, whether intended or not, to say that God had been faithful to Israel. *Either way*, to affirm that God's Covenantal dealings with Israel had been finished was to affirm that her eschaton had arrived and was past. Paul emphatically denied this.

[40] Technically, Jesus was the first fruit of the first fruits, in fulfillment of the first fruit typology found in Leviticus 23. There, you have the first fruit of barley, then, the first fruit of wheat, followed by harvest. This is the order of 1 Corinthians 15: Christ the first fruit of the first fruit, then the first fruits, then the harvest.

This issue is important. The *nature* of the resurrection of the *first fruits* saints who were part of the resurrection of whom Christ was *the first fruit*, clearly demands a non-physical resurrection. (Lest it be argued that I am implying a non-literal resurrection of Jesus, I deny this and affirm my conviction and belief in His physical resurrection. That was, however, a *sign* (John 20.30-31) and should never take precedent over what it *signified*. What we are affirming is that the Biblical emphasis on Christ's resurrection and the believer's emulation of that, is Christ's death "to sin," and His life, the eternal life with the Father (Romans 6.9f).

Those who appeal to 2 Timothy 2.17-19 to refute Covenant Eschatology are guilty of the worst sort of "proof-texting." They find a verse that *sounds* impressive and use it to their advantage without actually investigating the true interpretation of the text.

Those attempting to use this text to prove a yet future resurrection are failing to explain how anyone, given the literalistic interpretation of resurrection, could believe it had already happened.

They are ignoring the Biblically defined *time* for the resurrection, the first century. They take a text written just prior to the prophesied time of fulfillment and insist that if it was future it must be future *now*. The operative principle seems to be "once future, always future." That is a *hermeneutic of anachronism*.

They are ignoring the true context of the resurrection, the last days of Israel and the time of her judgment. I must take a moment to flesh this out.

They are ignoring Paul's earlier discussion of death and life (v. 11-12), which sets the context for his condemnation of Hymenaeus.

Please catch the power of this: you cannot affirm that God has finished His dealings with Israel without affirming the Day of the Lord and the resurrection have occurred. The Day of the Lord and resurrection belong to the Last Days of Israel,[41] not the last days of the church age. This critical

---

[41] See my book *The Last Days: Identified*, for proof that in the Bible, the term, *Last Days*, is referent to the end of

issue is missed, ignored or denied by the Amillennial and Postmillennial world and abused by the dispensational world. Let me illustrate.

Isaiah 25-27 – The resurrection of Isaiah is undeniably posited by YHVH at the time when the Lord would destroy the fortified city, and turn the temple over to strangers (25.1-3). The Day of the Lord, when "leviathan" i.e. the devil, would be destroyed, would be the day of Israel's salvation to be sure. However, it would also be when YHVH would also forsake and destroy the people He had created, when He destroyed the fortified city and turned the altar into chalk stone (27.9f).

Isaiah 64-66 posited the New Creation at the time when YHVH would destroy Old Covenant Israel: "The Lord God shall slay you, and call His people by another name" (65.13f).

Daniel 12 – Just as Isaiah, Daniel anticipated the resurrection and said it would be "when the power of the holy people is completely shattered" (v. 7).

I just have to briefly comment on Daniel 12 and the comments of Strimple. He claims Daniel 12 clearly predicted the end time resurrection of corpses out of the dirt and that Daniel is echoed in John 5.28-29. He says, "Also interesting are the gymnastics in which hyper-preterists must engage in order to avoid the clear teaching of these verses regarding one coming resurrection for all, both righteous and unrighteous" (*WSTTB*, 2004, 297).

What gymnastics "hyper-preterists" engage in, Strimple does not say. What he means by claiming preterists try to avoid the doctrine of one resurrection in Daniel is, well, baffling. I am personally unaware of any preterists that posit more than one resurrection in Daniel.

What is so interesting, however, is that Strimple is the one totally ignoring what Daniel said. Does he comment on the fact that the resurrection is tied inextricably to the Great Tribulation, an event that Jesus posited for his generation (Matthew 24.15-21)? Not a word. Does he inform us that Peter

---

the Old Covenant world of Israel, not the last days of the Christian age.

speaks of the salvation that was to come at the time of the end, and that he, Peter was living in the prophesied time (1 Peter 1.5-12, 20)? Not a whisper. Does he mention the "clear teaching" of Daniel 12.6-7 that so unequivocally posits that end of the age at the destruction of Old Covenant Israel, when the power of the holy people would be completely shattered? Not a syllable. So, the good Dr. Strimple is the one playing games with the text, not the true preterist.

Many other examples of the connection between the resurrection and the end of Israel's covenant age could be given, but this is sufficient. Why is this important, and what is the relevance to the issue of the Hymenaean Heresy question? It is important because not one of the futurist views of eschatology teach that at the end of the current age (the time of the resurrection) Israel is destroyed! Not one of them!

Amillennialists, as a general rule, say God was through with Israel at the cross. There are no eschatological promises concerning Israel to be fulfilled. In fact, on FaceBook,[42] as I write this, William Bell and I have been engaging in numerous written exchanges with several Amillennial ministers. The foundational doctrine they all espouse is that God was through with Israel at the Cross, that Torah passed at that time. This single issue is so foundational to Amillennialism, that if it is falsified, the entire paradigm falls to the ground.

Postmillennialists have no doctrine and no place for the future destruction of "the power of the holy people." Classical Postmillennialism says Israel is converted at the end of the Christian age– not destroyed.

Premillennialists likewise have no eschatology in which Israel is destroyed to create a new people and to bring in the New Creation.

Do you see the problem? All futurist eschatologies are in overt denial of a fundamental and undeniable Bible doctrine– eschatology belonged to Israel's last days. And, the eschatological consummation would only come

---

[42] The discussions, at least many of them, have taken place on the Facebook page "As It Is Written," owned by Steve Baisden.

when the Old Covenant world of Israel was swept away, giving way to the New Covenant world of Christ and his eternal kingdom (Hebrews 12.21-28).

So, when futurists condemn advocates of Covenant Eschatology for honoring the framework and time of the resurrection, the tragedy is, they are themselves guilty of positing the consummation at the entirely wrong place, the wrong time, and in fulfillment of the "wrong" prophecies, i.e. prophecies supposedly given to the church divorced from Israel.

> **As a general rule, those who appeal to 2 Timothy 2.17f to condemn true preterists are themselves guilty of positing the resurrection at the wrong place, the wrong time, and in fulfillment of the wrong prophecies!**

Hymenaeus at least had the framework and the imminence issues correct, even though he patently had the consummation occurring prematurely. Futurist eschatologies do not even have the time and framework correct, and yet, they condemn full preterists who are the only ones espousing the correct time and framework. Isn't there something horribly wrong with this scenario?

We continue now with our examination of the abuse of 2 Timothy 2 by those who cast aspersions on advocates of Covenant Eschatology.

They are failing to see how Paul's citation of the book of Numbers relates to the controversy with Hymenaeus.

They are failing to give proper import to the interconnectedness of the kingdom, parousia, judgment and the resurrection. They are failing to see that Jesus and Paul emphatically stated the kingdom and the resurrection were not optically discernable events.

To attempt to utilize 2 Timothy 2.17-19 to negate Covenant Eschatology is, therefore, unscholarly, specious and futile. The failure to honor the true issues at stake in 2 Timothy 2 and 2 Thessalonians 2, is leading to the false accusation of the resurrection of the *Hymenaean Heresy*. The proper understanding of these verses supports the AD 70 parousia and resurrection. We turn now to a demonstration of when the resurrection was to occur.

POINT #4
SEVENTY WEEKS ARE DETERMINED...
FOR THE RESURRECTION!!

My approach here is to discuss almost exclusively *the timing and framework* for the resurrection as determined in the great prophecy of Daniel 9.24f.[43] Of course, if one determines from scripture that the resurrection was to be in the first century, we must bring our concepts of the nature of the event– including our view of 1 Corinthians 15– into line with that time frame. After all: *Time Determines Nature*.

Other books do an excellent job of discussing 1 Corinthians 15 in an exegetical manner and I recommend the reader examine those works.[44] For the moment, to help the reader to understand my approach, I would reiterate an issue introduced above and that is the Biblical fact that the promise of the resurrection belonged to Israel. This is patently true and yet, essentially ignored, to varying degrees, by all futurist eschatologies.

That resurrection belonged to Israel is confirmed in 1 Corinthians 15. Paul, in predicting resurrection, said it would be the time when two Old Covenant prophecies, Isaiah 25.6-8 and Hosea 13.14, were fulfilled.[45] Now,

---

[43] For an in-depth examination of Daniel 9 and how it foretold the resurrection, see my *Seventy Weeks Are Determined...For the Resurrection*. This book demonstrates, as we will only briefly highlight here, that the constituent elements of Daniel 9 are resurrection motifs.

[44] Particularly, Max R. King's *The Cross and the Parousia, Two Aspects of One Age Changing Eschaton*. Also, Samuel Frost, *Essays on the Resurrection*.

[45] As a hermeneutical exercise, it should be noted that neither Isaiah 25 nor Hosea 13 contain a hint of a physical resurrection. Both passages deal with "sin-death" i.e. alienation from God because of sin. Since Paul says the resurrection he anticipated would be when "the law" that is "the strength of sin" (i.e. the Mosaic Law), was removed and the sting of death, i.e. sin, overcome (1 Corinthians 15.54-56) and since he said the resurrection would be when the predictions of Isaiah and Hosea were fulfilled, this is *prima*

since resurrection would be the fulfillment of the promises made to Israel, then, to determine definitively when all of God's promises to Israel were, or will be, fulfilled, is to irrefutably determine when resurrection would occur.

> **My purpose is to demonstrate with clarity and an abundance of evidence, what the Bible says about the time and the framework for the resurrection. The evidence is clear, emphatic and powerful!**

I understand that most who read this book have been raised to believe the resurrection is the raising of human corpses out of the ground.[46] However, *that doctrine is not true*. Resurrection is the restoration of the life lost in Adam: "As in Adam all men die, even so in Christ shall all men be made alive" (1 Corinthians 15.22). The life lost in Adam was not physical life and the death introduced by Adam was not physical death. The death introduced by Adam was sin-death, the loss of fellowship with God. We cannot develop this at length here. See my book for a full development of this.[47]

Our purpose here is to show unmistakably what the Bible says about the time and the framework for the resurrection. We will not discuss a lot of questions about the resurrection because although those issues are

---

facie proof Paul was not predicting a resurrection from physical death. The prophecies he cites are predictions of resurrection from sin-death and the frame-work he gives is deliverance from sin-death. There is no hint of a physical resurrection here.

[46] I was raised as a fifth generation Amillennialist in the churches of Christ. The Amillennial view says the resurrection is at the end of the church age, at the end of time. It was a total shock to me to discover that the Bible is emphatic in teaching the Christian age has no end.

[47] Don K. Preston, *We Shall Meet Him in the Air, The Wedding of the King of kings*, for a full discussion of the nature of the death of Adam.

important, the focus of this work is confined to what the Bible says about the *when* of the resurrection.

Lots of good, honest Bible believers are totally unaware of the time problem in the Bible. By that we mean while the Bible is very plain as to when the Second Coming, the judgment and resurrection were to occur, many Bible believers are unaware of those time statements[48] or in some cases, they have tuned them out because they don't have the answers.[49] If Christ said He was coming back in the first century, did He not keep his word? How can we believe in Jesus if He lied or failed, or was mistaken? Is the Bible really inspired if the apostles and Biblical writers said the end of the age was coming in the first century and it did not happen?

As a matter of fact, if the Bible writers were wrong, the Bible is not inspired. It is that simple. If Jesus said He was coming back in his generation but He did not come back, He is not the Son of God. There is no way out of that conundrum. The only way to honor the Bible and maintain the deity of Jesus is to maintain He kept his word and the Bible writers were right. The end of the age did come. Christ did come in judgment. The resurrection did occur.

If you were raised in one of the traditional views of eschatology, you are probably saying, "How could this be? How could Christ have come? Did every eye see him?" For answers to these questions and more, we direct you to some of our other writings that discuss the nature of Christ's coming.[50]

---

[48] See my *Can God Tell Time?* for an-depth study of God and time. There is no question that in scripture, God communicated truthfully and unambiguously about time, as a general rule.

[49] I have personally studied with many ministers who told me that in their years of ministry, when they came on the time statements about the first century imminence of the end, they "did the passover" i.e. they simply "passed over" the texts because they did know how to deal with them.

[50] Be sure to see my book *Like Father Like Son, On Clouds of Glory*. This major work demonstrates beyond a

The purpose of this section, as just noted, is to focus on what the Bible says about *when the resurrection was to occur.* The framework for the resurrection was the last days of Old Covenant Israel, not the last days of time. The time for the resurrection was to be the time of the judgment of Jerusalem in AD 70.

As I stated at the outset, my focus is the *framework* and the *time* of the resurrection as set forth in scripture. My thoughts will be drawn from and based on the great seventy week prophecy of Daniel 9.[51] My premise is simple:

1. Daniel 9.24f is not in any way concerned with the end of the Christian age and by and large, this is admitted by the partial preterists. As Gentry says, "The prophecy's focus is on Israel."[52] In *WSTTB*, (220+) Kistemaker *seems* to take a position that is actually fatal. He agrees "the holy city" in Daniel was referent to Old Covenant Jerusalem. This would seem therefore, to demand the seventy weeks are concerned with Israel and Old Covenant Jerusalem.

However, when he comes to the NT, he changes that designation to the church. But if, and I emphasize the "if," he is utilizing the term "the holy city" of Daniel to then refer to the church, this demands the seventy weeks are not fulfilled until the so called end of time. Furthermore, it demands that the church is the object of the Abomination of Desolation and the overwhelming flood of destruction of Daniel 9! This is patently false.

---

shadow of a doubt that Christ never promised to come back literally, bodily and in an optically visible manner.

[51] I presented some of the material in this book in public formal debate with Thomas Thrasher, March 13, 2004, in Indianapolis, Indiana. The impact of the material was very positive. I have now expanded that material into a larger book, *Seventy Weeks Are Determined...For the Resurrection*.

[52] Kenneth Gentry, *He Shall Have Dominion*, (Tyler, TX, Institute for Christian Economics, 1992)329+.

2. The seventy week prophecy of Daniel 9 was completely fulfilled in the first century.[53] There is a consensus among partial preterists that this is true.[54]

3. If, therefore, I can prove that Daniel 9 is a prediction of the resurrection from the dead, I will have proven the resurrection is past.

It may be objected at the outset that Daniel 9 does not mention the word "resurrection" and of course this is true. However, as I will show, the specific word does not have to appear for the doctrine to appear.[55] Further, the promised blessings of Daniel 9 are motifs inextricably linked to resurrection. Therefore, while the *word* "resurrection" is not found in Daniel 9.24f, the *doctrine* definitely is.

Daniel was told, "Seventy weeks are determined on your people and for your holy city, to finish the transgression, to make an end of sins, to make reconciliation for iniquity, to bring in everlasting righteousness, to seal up vision and prophecy and to anoint the Most Holy." While there are six elements of promise, we will focus on only four.

---

[53] Keith Mathison, *Postmillennialism: And Eschatology of Hope,* (New Jersey, P and R Publishing, 1999)220, "Traditionally, the church has interpreted this prophecy in Daniel as a prophecy of the first advent of Christ and the destruction of Jerusalem by the Roman armies."

[54] See Gary DeMar, *Last Days Madness*, (Atlanta, American Vision, 1994)231f; Lorraine Boettner, *The Millennium*, (Philadelphia, Presbyterian and Reformed Press, 1957) 224+; (Gentry, *Dominion*, 329f).

[55] There is a horrid hermeneutic running amok in evangelical Christianity that says if a given word is not present in a text, or even if different words are used from text to text, that this means the texts cannot be speaking of a given subject, or the same subject. To suggest that a writer must include every word, every tenet associated with a given doctrine, every time he mentions that doctrine is false and cannot be sustained. See my debate with Joel McDurmon, July, 2012, for a discussion of this hermeneutic.

One cannot extend the fulfillment of these promises beyond the seventy weeks. To suggest for instance that while seventy weeks were determined "to make atonement for sin" the actual atonement would not occur for thousands of years beyond the terminus *(ad quem,* i.e. the end), of the seventy weeks is to ignore the parameters of the time "determined."

Gentry notes the millennial attempt to extend the seventy weeks 2000 years beyond the atoning work of Jesus, "The Dispensationalists here prefers to interpret this result as *application* rather than effecting. He sees it as subjective appropriation instead of objective accomplishment." Gentry counters by observing, "On the basis of the Hebrew verb, the passage clearly speaks of the actual *making reconciliation* (or *atonement)."* *(Dominion,* 315, his emphasis) The import of Gentry's point is great for the Millennialists. The Atonement promised in Daniel 9 was the *objective appropriation of Atonement,* the "cultic actions of the Atonement in the passion of Jesus. If the Millennialists posit the end of the seventieth week as yet future, the accomplishment of the Atonement has not even been made.

The problem for Gentry, however, is he has the atonement accomplished before the time posited by Scripture.

If the elements of Daniel 9.24 were not to be fulfilled *within the determined* seventy *weeks,* what was the point of saying, "Seventy weeks are determined on your people and on your holy city"? The significance of this will become more apparent as we proceed. Keep this vital fact in mind.

SEVENTY WEEKS ARE DETERMINED: "TO PUT AN END TO SIN"

Gentry and Mathison believe the prediction "to put away sin" is unrelated to Christ's redemptive work, but rather means, "Israel's sins were reserved for punishment until the generation of the Messiah." (Mathison, *1999*, 221) Gentry claims the term means, "The sealing or reserving of the sins indicates that *within* the 'seventy weeks' Israel will complete her transgressions *and* with the completing of her sin, by crucifying Christ, God will act to reserve (*beyond the seventy weeks*) her sins for judgment." (*Dominion*, 315, his emphasis). There are several problems with this view.

First, I have been unable to find translational support for the idea of "reserving Israel's sins for judgment." I have gone through my shelves of Bible translations and by far, the most common rendering of Daniel 9 is "put an end to sin." Not one renders the text "reserve sin for judgment."[56]

Second, Gentry's posit violates the text of Daniel 9. He says Israel's sin would be filled up and reserved for judgment, but the judgment lies outside the seventy weeks. This is *not* what Daniel was told. He was told, "Seventy weeks are determined on your people and on your city." *He was not told*, "Seventy weeks are determined to determine the fate of your city."[57]

---

[56] Among the translations were, ASV, NASV; RSV; NRSV; LXX; Douay; Amplified; New Jerusalem; KJV; NKJV, just to name a few.

[57] See my *Seal Up Vision and Prophecy* for a fuller discussion of the meaning of "is determined." Gentry and Mathison are saying the seventy weeks were set aside for the determination of the fate of Jerusalem. Again, this is false, because *the fate of the city is actually determined in Daniel 9*: "the people of the prince that shall come shall destroy the city and the sanctuary" (V. 26). So, it was not the fate of the city to be determined in the seventy weeks. The seventy weeks were allotted by God *for the fulfillment of the fate that had been determined in Daniel.*

Third, it is wrong to say Israel completely filled up the measure of her sin by crucifying Christ, although of course it is naturally tempting to do so. While Matthew 21 posits the killing of the Son as "the straw that broke the camel's back," Jesus added additional information in Matthew 23. As He stood in the temple and recounted Israel's long history of persecuting the righteous, Jesus said, "fill up then the measure of your father's guilt." (Matthew 23.32). How were they going to finally fill up that measure of sin? Verse 34 has the answer: "Behold, I send unto you prophets, wise men and scribes. Some of them you will crucify and some of them you will scourge in your synagogues and persecute from city to city." Israel would finally fill up the measure of her sin by persecuting the apostles and prophets sent by Jesus and this was patently after the Cross.

Paul concurred in this in 1 Thessalonians 2.15f, when speaking of the internecine Jewish history he said they, "killed both the Lord Jesus and their own prophets and have persecuted us and they do not please God and are contrary to all men, forbidding us to speak to the Gentiles that they may be saved, so as always to fill up the measure of their sins, but wrath has come upon them to the uttermost." Take note that for Paul, the filling up of the measure of Israel's sin was a then still ongoing process that had not yet reached its fullness.

Thus, the assertion that Israel would fill the measure of her sin at the Cross and God would at that time "reserve her for punishment" *after the* seventy *weeks* is untenable. The filling up of the measure of Israel's sins extends *well beyond* the time when most partial preterists say it occurred. Yet, according to Daniel, the filling up of the measure of sin (i.e. the finishing of transgressions), belongs to the seventy weeks. And, it must not be forgotten that Daniel was told, "seventy weeks are determined... on your holy city." The fate of the city lies within the seventy weeks just as surely as "finishing the transgression" lies within the seventy weeks.

Paul emphatically said it was his suffering that was filling up, "what is lacking in the afflictions of Christ" (Colossians 1.24f). O'Brien says: "The presence of the definite article τά suggests that the phrase 'what is lacking in Christ's afflictions,' refers to something well known and agrees with the apocalyptic notion of a definite measure of affliction to be endured in the last days. As God had set a definite measure in time (Mk. 13.5-27) and the limit of the tribulations at the end, so there is a definite measure of suffering that is to be filled up. That limit of messianic woes has not yet been reached. There are still deficiencies which Paul through his sufferings is in the process of completing."[58]

Very clearly, for Paul, the measure of sin was not yet full. Paul believed that fullness was to be achieved in his personal tribulation and that of the apostolate, "God has displayed us, the apostles, last, as men condemned to death" (1 Corinthians 4.9). Historically, myriads have died after Paul and the other apostles. That was not Paul's concern. He was focused on the eschatological "measured suffering" and corollary "measure of sin."

Now, since the suffering of Paul and the apostolate are undeniably post Cross, it cannot be argued that Israel filled up the measure of her sin (i.e. finished the transgression) at the Cross. This falsifies the partial preterist view that "putting away of sin" is referent to "reserving the fate" as a result of filling the measure of sin and then reserving punishment until after the seventy weeks. If the filling up of the measure of sin extends beyond the time posited by Mathison and Gentry, and it surely does, their paradigm is false.

There is a consensus that "putting away of sin" is referent to the atoning work of Jesus. The Hebrew writer says Christ appeared "to put away sin" (9.26) and this theme of "putting away of sin" in fulfillment of God's promises to Israel is found throughout the New Testament. Furthermore, *the time of the putting away of sin is the time of the resurrection.*

In 1 Corinthians 15 we find Paul's great discourse on the resurrection and in verses 23f he says Christ had "put all things under his feet." The last enemy to be (literally, *being*[59]) destroyed, Paul says, "is (the) death." And

---

[58] Peter O'Brien, *Word Biblical Commentary, Colossians and Philemon* (Waco, Word Publishers, 1982)80.

[59] In 1 Corinthians 15 and Paul's discussion of the resurrection, he repeatedly uses the *present passive indicative* and the *present active indicative*. These Greek active tenses have troubled the commentators. E.G. Gordon Fee, *NICNT, The First Epistle to the Corinthians*, (Grand Rapids, Eerdmans, 1987)756. And well they should be troubled, for

when would death be conquered? It would be when "the sting of death," *sin*, would be finally put under Christ. Thus, the resurrection would be when the sting of death would be put down by Christ. But the sting of death is sin (1 Corinthians 15.55-56). Therefore, resurrection would be when sin would be put down by Christ. That leads to our initial argument from Daniel 9:

The time of the putting away of sin belongs to the seventy weeks of Daniel 9.24f.

But, the time of the resurrection would be when sin was put away (1 Corinthians 15.55-56).

Therefore, the time of the resurrection, the time of the putting away of sin, belongs to the seventy weeks of Daniel 9.24f.

Let me follow that with this:

The seventy weeks of Daniel 9.24f ended with the fall of Jerusalem in AD 70.[60]

But the time of the resurrection belongs to the seventy weeks of Daniel 9.24f.

---

unless there is powerful evidence to demand the present passive tenses, their presence means that Paul believed the resurrection of which he wrote was already underway!

[60] Most partial preterists have the seventy weeks ending with the stoning of Stephen, or the conversion of the Gentiles. See my *Seal Up Vision and Prophecy*, or my *Seventy Weeks Are Determined...For the Resurrection*, for a full discussion of why these proposals are untenable. Simply stated, where ever one posits the termination of the seventy weeks, it is at that point that resurrection, i.e. the putting away of sin, occurs. Thus, if one places the putting away of sin at the Cross, per Gentry, Mathison, etc, you must place resurrection there as well.

Therefore, the resurrection belongs to the time of the fall of Jerusalem in AD 70.

At this juncture it is vital to be reminded that *Paul's resurrection doctrine was the hope of Israel.* This issue is all but totally ignored by the contributors to *WSTTB*.[61] Their failure to honor and discuss this fact is fatal to their entire effort.

Notice our next chart showing the correlation between Daniel 9 and 1 Corinthians 15. Both deal with the fulfillment of God's promises to Israel. Both give a time referent for fulfillment.

---

[61] Mathison gives lip service to this issue, stating: "Old Testament eschatology is fundamentally grounded in God's covenant with Israel." (2004, 157). However, he sees OT eschatology as almost exclusively typological of the final Day of the Lord *at the end of human history-* not in fulfillment of OT prophecy, and promises made to Israel (p. 159). See my *AD 70: A Shadow of the "Real" End?* for a thorough refutation of this concept.

Daniel 9	1 Corinthians 15
Time of the end (v. 27)	Time of the end (v. 23f)
Time of the kingdom (cf. Lk. 21.31)	Time of the kingdom (v. 50f)
Putting away of sin (v. 24)	Putting away of sin (v. 23f; 54f)
End of Old Covenant age	End of Old Covenant age (v. 54-56).[62]
Fulfillment of OT promises to Israel (v. 24)	Fulfillment of OT promises to Israel (v. 54f)
Consummated in AD 70 (v. 27)	"We shall not all sleep" (v. 50)

Daniel 9 and 1 Corinthians 15 are clearly speaking of the same time and the same event, the resurrection. But, once again, the contributors to *WSTTB* totally ignore this relationship and the direct parallels. Instead, Pratt speaks of the failure of fulfillment of Daniel 9 (2004, 145), while Mathison posits fulfillment (2004, 163), but, neither man sees the relationship between Daniel 9 and the resurrection.

---

[62] Paul said the resurrection would be when "the law" that was "the strength of sin" was removed. In Paul, the term "the law," when used without modifiers, (110 times), is invariably the law of Moses. Thus, resurrection would be when the Old Covenant was removed. Those who posit the resurrection at the end of the Christian age must view the gospel of Christ is the strength of sin, since resurrection is when "the Law" (the strength of sin), will be removed. Thus, if the resurrection is at the end of this (gospel) age and the strength of sin (the law) is removed at the end of the age, this means the gospel is called the strength of sin. This hardly agrees with Paul's assessment in Romans 8.1f. See my 2008 formal debate with Mac Deaver. He affirmed that the gospel is in fact the strength of sin.

The connections between Daniel 9 and Corinthians are precise and perfect. This being true, since Daniel 9 posits the resurrection at the end of the Old Covenant world of Israel, this demands that 1 Corinthians 15 was fulfilled in the demise of the "world" and the Law that was "the strength of sin."

Notice the correlation with Hebrews 9.26: "Now, once, at the end of the ages He has appeared, to put away sin, by the sacrifice of himself." Make no mistake about this critical fact: "Jesus Christ has become the servant to the circumcision to confirm the promises made to the fathers" (Romans 15.8). He came to minister to Israel, his people, to seek that which was lost (Matthew 15.10f) and to fulfill His Father's promises to them. Thus, when the writer says Christ came to "put away sin" we should not look anywhere else than the promises God made to Israel to determine the nature and framework of Christ's work. He came to put away sin, in fulfillment of God's promises to Israel.

Where did the Hebrew writer get the idea of "putting away of sin?" Could he have gotten that idea from Daniel 9.24? And notice, just as Daniel 9 anticipated the putting away of sin in the consummation of God's determined time on the people and the city, Jesus appeared at "the end of the ages" (*suntelia ton aionion*)[63] to put away sin. The end of the seventy weeks would be the end of the age, *Israel's age.* And once again, this crucial fact is ignored by the contributors to *WSTTB*. Instead of honoring the Biblical datum, they arbitrarily identify the end of the age as the end of the Christian age, and the end of time, neither of which is a Biblical doctrine.

Jesus appeared, during the last days of that Old Covenant age (Galatians 4.4; Hebrews 1.1-2), to accomplish what Daniel 9 foretold for the last days: The putting away of sin. This is not just coincidental usage of language. This is not just similarity of language. Hebrews is discussing what Daniel foretold.

---

[63] See my *Into All the World, Then Comes the End*, for a fuller discussion of this distinctive Greek term. It is only used six times in scriptures and invariably refers to the end of the Old Covenant world of Israel.

Jesus did not appear at the end of the Christian age to put away sin. Jesus came to put away sin, just as Daniel said seventy weeks were determined to put away sin. The Messiah was to die "after the sixty ninth week" (Daniel 9.26). The Passion was the power by which the removal of sin began. He triumphed over his enemies in the Cross (Colossians 2.15f), but the parousia would be the consummation of the process begun (cf. 1 Corinthians 15.21-28; Philippians 1.6).[64] This is the "already-but-not-yet" of the putting away of sin. But remember, Daniel said only seventy weeks were determined to put away sin. He did not say the process would begin within the seventy weeks but not be consummated for 2000 years.

If the putting away of sin is the time of the resurrection and if seventy weeks were determined to put away sin, it must be true the resurrection must be confined to and fulfilled by the time of the completion of the seventy weeks. Not one of the authors in *WSTTB* even remotely addresses this issue.

If the partial preterists were to argue that the initiation of the putting away of sins began within the seventy weeks, but the consummation has not yet taken place, because the resurrection, per their paradigm has not occurred, they are guilty of inserting a 2000 year gap in the text of Daniel 9. But Daniel 9 does not say, nor indicate that seventy weeks were determined to start a process that would not be completed for two millennia. It says "Seventy weeks are determined on your people and on your holy city...to

---

[64] Some people, wrongly in my opinion, try to negate the significance of Christ's end of the age parousia in AD 70 by claiming preterists negate the importance of the Passion by focusing on the parousia. This "dodge" fails to understand that, as Max King pointed out so well in his tome, *The Cross and the Parousia*, these two events were part of one age changing period. There is an inextricable link between the Cross and the parousia. You cannot say one is substantively more important than the other, except in the relationship between initiation and consummation. From passion to parousia was a *singular eschaton*, an organic unity, just as the building of an edifice. Can one say which is the more important, foundation or finish? Without any question, the passion is the foundation. Yet, to depreciate the parousia is an egregious error.

put away sin." This means that unless resurrection is totally unrelated to the promise of putting away of sin, the resurrection had to have occurred by the end of the seventy weeks, in AD 70.

To Make An Atonement For Sin

There is no disagreement, in any conservative commentary, that this is referent to the atoning work of Jesus Christ. The tragedy is, the great majority of commentaries stop the atoning process at the Cross, whereas Scripture posits the consummation of the Atonement at the parousia of Christ. Gentry says of the promise to make an atonement for sin, "It clearly speaks of Christ's atoning death, which is the ultimate atonement to which all the temple rituals looked (Hebrews 9.26). This also occurred during his earthly ministry – at his death." (*Dominion*, 315). Mathison likewise argues: "This was fulfilled in Christ's atoning death." (*1999*, 221).

Gentry is correct to say Christ's atoning death is what all the temple rituals looked toward. Furthermore, *Christ's high priestly function*, in offering himself as a sacrifice, is also pointed to by those Old Covenant rituals. It is here the partial preterists and all futurists abandon the text.

Notice the chart that shows the direct type/anti-type relationship between Jesus in His High Priestly service and of the Old Covenant High Priest on the Day of Atonement.

O.T. HIGH PRIEST ON DAY OF ATONEMENT	CHRIST, HIGH PRIEST TO MAKE ATONEMENT
PRIEST KILLED THE SACRIFICE	CHRIST APPEARED TO "PUT AWAY SIN" BY HIS SACRIFICE (9.26)
PRIEST ENTERED THE MOST HOLY PLACE	"CHRIST ENTERED THE HOLY PLACE" (9.24)
RETURN OF HIGH PRIEST FROM MHP FINISHED ATONEMENT & DECLARED SALVATION	TO THOSE WHO EAGERLY LOOK FOR HIM, HE SHALL APPEAR A SECOND TIME, FOR SALVATION (9.28)

It will be noted that after describing these actions by Christ, so perfectly picturing the Old Covenant Day of Atonement, the writer of Hebrews says Christ would appear a second time... "*for* the law, having a shadow of good things to come, can never by those sacrifices which they make year by year continually, perfect" (Hebrews 10.1). In other words, the Old Law and its typological functions were a shadow and Christ in his High Priestly function was the fulfillment. Just as the High Priest killed the sacrifice, entered the Most Holy Place and came back out, Jesus offered himself and entered the Most Holy Place and was set to "appear the second time, for salvation, *for* the law having a shadow of good things about to come...". It was necessary for the fulfillment of the Old Covenant liturgical praxis that Christ fulfill every aspect of the High Priest's Atoning function and that included the coming out of the Most Holy Place to declare the Atonement accepted. Simply stated, if the High Priest did not come back out of the Most Holy Place, *there was no Atonement.*

However, virtually all futurist paradigms say the Atonement was finished *at the Cross*. This in spite of the fact Christ's Priestly function *demanded* entrance into the Most Holy and then the return from the Most Holy Place before the Atonement was finished. This leads to the following argument:

The Atonement work of Christ would be perfected and consummated at his "Second Coming" (Hebrews 9.28).

But the Second Coming is the time of the resurrection of the dead (1 Corinthians 15).

Therefore, the Atonement work of Christ would be perfected at the resurrection of the dead.

Consider this, following on that:

The Atonement work of Christ would be perfected at the resurrection of the dead.

But the seventy weeks were determined to make the Atonement (Daniel 9.24).

Therefore, the resurrection of the dead, at the perfection of the Atonement work of Jesus, would occur within, or by the end of, the seventy weeks.

I would observe that those who posit the completion of the Atonement at the cross are guilty of destroying the chronological sequence of the festal calendar of Israel that lies behind so much of the NT and particularly Hebrews. While Passover– Christ's death on the cross– was considered a preliminary to the Atonement, the Day of Atonement belonged to the last of Israel's three feast days, that occurred in the fall, as opposed to the beginning of the year. For brevity, I can only make a basic observation.

Hebrews 9f is patently about the fulfillment of the typological Day of Atonement praxis. As such, that discussion must be viewed from the perspective of the eschatological consummation. In Hebraic thought, the last three feast days foreshadowed the Judgment (Rosh Ha Shanah, the Feast of Trumpets), followed by Yom Kippur (Day of Atonement) and finally the Feast of Succot, or the Feast of Harvest, that anticipated the resurrection.

The point is that Yom Kippur occurred in the midst of the final three feasts. As Callaway says, the Jews believed, "Yom Kippur (Day of Atonement, DKP) is the culmination of Rosh Ha Shanah."[65] Well, if the Day of Atonement was the culmination of *the Feast of Trumpets*, i.e. the Day of Judgment, how in the name of reason – or with any consistent relationship with chronological sequence – can it be argued that the Atonement was finalized at the very first of the seven feasts? That is anachronistic, to say the very least.

We should be reminded that, "On the basis of the Hebrew verb, the passage (Daniel 9.24, DKP) clearly speaks of the actual making of reconciliation (or atonement) (*Dominion*, 351). It cannot therefore, be argued that Christ made the atonement within the seventy weeks, but the application lies outside those parameters.[66] Gentry agrees, "The seventy weeks necessarily includes the effecting of this result, as well."(*Weeks*, 6). The idea of a gap between appropriation and application is, after all, the millennial view

---

[65] Jared Callaway, *The Sabbath and Sanctuary*, (Tubingen, Germany, Mohr Siebeck, 2013)166.

[66] This is not to say by any means, the benefits of the Atonement are not applicable today, for any and all men who would come into the blessings of Israel's fulfilled redemption story. It is simply to honor the fact that the language of Daniel refers to the "cultic" actions of making the atonement.

rejected by Gentry and most partial preterists. Yet, strangely enough, a gap is precisely what the Postmillennialists must have to posit resurrection beyond AD 70.

Unless one can prove definitively that the consummation of the Atonement was unrelated to the coming of the High Priest out of the Most Holy Place, it is *prima facie* proof that the Atonement was not completed until that "return." But, if the Atonement was not completed until the High Priest came out of the Most Holy Place, this is indisputable proof that the parousia, to complete the Atonement, is confined to the seventy weeks of Daniel 9.24. Since the "Second Coming" is the time of the resurrection, the resurrection must have occurred by the end of the seventy weeks of Daniel 9.24.

Take note again how Mathison, Gentry, DeMar and others argue that the seventy weeks actually ended circa 35 AD while the destruction of Jerusalem was only "determined" within the Heptads. However, the Atonement refutes that idea.

The Atonement would not be complete until the coming of the High Priest out of the Most Holy Place (Hebrews 9.28). The Atonement belongs, *totally*, to the seventy weeks. You cannot have the Atonement *initiated* within the Heptads and then *consummated* outside those parameters, without denying the text of Daniel 9. However, since the coming of the High Priest was still in the future from Hebrews 9 – yet was coming in "a very, very little while" (10.37) – this means the seventy weeks had not been consummated years before. And, since the coming of Christ out of the Most Holy is set within the context of the imminent judgment of Israel (Hebrews 10.26-37), this means the resurrection, the consummation of the Atonement and the seventy weeks, was to occur in that judgment.

The only way to negate this argument is to argue:
1) That the making of Atonement is unrelated to the "final coming" of Christ at the time of the resurrection. Yet, Hebrews 9 posits the "Second Coming" which is universally posited as the time of the resurrection, as the time when the Atonement would be perfected. Atonement was not finished without the return of the High Priest. That would be a violation of the type/anti-type *imagery* and the *text* of Hebrews 9.

2) That the Atonement was made within the seventy weeks, but it would/will be *applied* at the parousia. This is the Millennial view that partial preterists vehemently deny. The problem is there is no textual justification for this argument in Daniel.

> **Seventy weeks were determined to make the Atonement.**
>
> **The consummation of the Atonement process is the parousia, at the time of the resurrection.**
>
> **Therefore, the resurrection is confined to the seventy weeks of Daniel 9.**

3) That the making of the Atonement in Daniel 9 is unrelated to the High Priestly Atonement work of Jesus in Hebrews 9. Yet it is from the typological Old Covenant world of Daniel's promise of the Atonement that the Hebrew writer makes his argument about Christ's Atoning work.

If in fact the Hebrew writer is writing about the consummation of the Atonement work of Christ (and of course this is indisputable) and if the Atoning work of Christ is the Atonement promised by Daniel, then the consummation of Christ's Atonement work is confined to the seventy weeks of Daniel 9. But, the consummation of Christ's Atonement work is the Second Coming, i.e. the time of the resurrection. Therefore, the resurrection is confined to the seventy weeks of Daniel 9.

The bottom line is, whereever you posit the consummated work of Christ's Atonement, it is there where you place the finishing of the seventy weeks of Daniel 9. And, where ever you place the consummation of Christ's Atonement work, it is *there* you place resurrection. If the resurrection has not occurred, *the seventy weeks are not yet fulfilled*. If the seventy weeks are fulfilled, meaning Christ's Atonement work is perfected, resurrection has occurred.

TO BRING IN EVERLASTING RIGHTEOUSNESS

Gentry says: "The final, complete atonement establishes righteousness. This speaks of the objective accomplishment, not the subjective appropriation of righteousness." (*Dominion*, 316) We agree, but unfortunately, partial preterists once again stop short of proper application. Contra Gentry, Mathison, etc. it is clear the New Testament writers were still awaiting the consummation of the work of righteousness and did not see that work as finished at the Cross.

Notice the problem with Gentry's posit.
"The final, complete atonement establishes righteousness." (Gentry).

But the New Testament saints were "eagerly awaiting the hope of righteousness" (Galatians 5.5).

Therefore, the New Testament saints were eagerly awaiting "the final complete atonement."

Now, since the first century saints were still awaiting the full arrival of the world of righteousness, the world that would be accomplished through the finished atonement, this is a definitive refutation of the view of Gentry, Mathison, DeMar, et. al, that the Atonement was finished at the Cross. If the atonement was finished at the Cross, the first century saints had no reason to be still eagerly awaiting "the new heavens and earth wherein dwells righteousness" (2 Peter 3.13).

Paul said, "We through the Spirit, eagerly await the hope of righteousness" (Galatians 5.5). The context makes it clear Paul was contrasting the futility of the Old Law and the world that could never give righteousness (Galatians 3.20f) with the Gospel of Jesus Christ that does give righteousness and life. The High Priestly atoning work of the Old Covenant priests could never offer enough sacrifices to make the worshiper perfect (Hebrews 10.1-4). That Law, that ministry, could never provide righteousness. The finished work of Christ in his High Priestly sacrifice, entrance into the Most Holy, and return, did make that perfect Atonement, however.

Furthermore, Paul says it was "through the Spirit" they were "eagerly" (from *apekdekomai*) awaiting the full arrival of that righteousness. It was that eschatological work of the Spirit that was guaranteeing the completion of the work begun (Colossians 1.12-13). This waiting through the Spirit is referent to the charismata, since it was that miraculous Spirit transforming (from *metamorphe*) the early church "from glory to glory" i.e. from the Old Covenant glory to the New (2 Corinthians 3.12-16). In Galatians 3f Paul reminds them it was that miraculous Spirit "perfecting" them in Christ, not through the Law.

The point is that it was the covenantal change from the Old Law to the New taking place and this is precisely the point of Daniel 9.24f. It would be the atoning work of Jesus the Messiah that would bring about the New Covenant world of "everlasting righteousness," not the end of the Christian age.

For Paul, that new world was not yet completed. The New Jerusalem had not yet descended from above and the Old World had not yet been cast out (Galatians 3.23f; 4.22f). The New Creation, wherein, "neither circumcision nor uncircumcision avails," had been born, but it was not yet perfected. Thus, they were still waiting for the bringing in of "everlasting righteousness," the full arrival of the New Creation. This is one of the reasons why it was so dangerous for Hymenaeus to say the resurrection was past.

Remember, Hymenaeus could argue that Paul himself said the New Creation had arrived– 2 Corinthians 5.17: "If any man is in Christ, he is a new creation." He could point to Romans 6, Ephesians 2 and 4, or at least Paul's sermons, where Paul spoke of the New Man foretold by the Old Covenant prophets. Had not Paul spoken of those things in the "past tense"?

Hymenaeus was clearly aware of the "already" of Paul's eschatology. However, he was cutting short the necessary consummation and perfection of that end times drama.

Peter also believed the new temple of God[67] was already under construction (1 Peter 2.5). He was eagerly "looking for (*prosdokao*) and hastening the Day of the Lord," and the arrival of "the new heavens and earth wherein dwells righteousness" as promised by the Old Covenant prophets (2 Peter 3.1-2, 13). Was the world of righteousness eagerly awaited by Peter different from that foretold by Daniel 9?

Furthermore, was Peter eagerly anticipating a different world of righteousness, from that being eagerly anticipated *by the Galatians*? Just how would one dichotomize between those two worlds of righteousness being eagerly anticipated by the first century saints? And don't forget, as Gentry correctly notes, it was the arrival of righteousness that would consummate the atonement. Thus, to delay the arrival of the world of righteousness being eagerly awaited in Galatians or 2 Peter 3, *is to delay the finished atonement*. But to delay the finished atonement delays the fulfillment of the seventy weeks of Daniel 9.

Most commentators are agreed that Peter's referent to the new heavens and earth is taken directly from Isaiah 65. This being true, it must be true Peter was anticipating the new creation to follow the judgment on Israel, for that is exactly what Isaiah 65 taught.

---

[67] There is considerable debate as to the identity of the "Most Holy" to be anointed during the seventy weeks of Daniel 9.24. Many partial preterists believe it is referent to the anointing of Christ at his baptism. (Mathison, *1999*, 221). Keil and Delitzsch note however, that the words used of this anointing are never used of persons, but of objects, and cultic objects of the temple at that. Keil and Delitzsch *Daniel*, (Grand Rapids, Eerdmans, 1975)349. (This may not be totally true, however). While there is no doubt Christ was "the anointed one," the idea seems to be that seventy weeks were determined to anoint the Most Holy of the new temple. This conforms to the prediction of the destruction of the "city and *sanctuary*" of 9.26. At the end of the seventy weeks, JHVH would remove the Old Most Holy, and anoint the new temple of Messiah. The idea of the passing of the old temple and the anticipation of the completion of the new Most Holy temple of Messiah permeates New Testament theology.

We should point out that some partial preterists argue that Isaiah 65, 2 Peter 3 and Revelation 21 foretold different New Creations. This is really quite incredible.

Gentry (*Dominion*, 1992, 363) delineates between Isaiah 65 and 2 Peter 3. Interestingly however, he says Revelation 21.2-5: "Is the bride of Christ that came down from God to replace the earthly Jerusalem in the first century. With the shaking and destruction of the old Jerusalem in AD 70, the heavenly (re-created) Jerusalem replaced her." But, if Revelation 21.1f is referent to the events of AD 70, *then since they follow the millennium, Gentry is forced to say that the millennium ended in AD 70!* Furthermore, if Revelation 21f is AD 70 that means that it is referent to the arrival of "everlasting righteousness" of Daniel 9. That in turn demands that the seventieth week ended in AD 70 -- not 35 years earlier as Gentry suggests.

Isaiah foretold that the new creation would come when Israel filled the measure of her sin (v. 6-8) and was destroyed, "the Lord God will destroy you and call His people by a new name" (v. 13f). As a consequence of that destruction, YHVH would, "create a new heavens and a new earth" (v. 17). So, if 2 Peter 3 was predicting the arrival of the world of righteousness foretold by Isaiah 65, he was anticipating the destruction of Old Covenant Israel, followed by the New Covenant World of Messiah.

Is this not what Daniel 9 predicted? Daniel foretold the consummation of Israel's Old Covenant existence and the New Covenant work of Messiah. But, the consummation of Israel's history meant the destruction of "the city and sanctuary" (Daniel 9.26). So, Daniel and Isaiah foretold the arrival of the new world of righteousness – the new heavens and earth – at the time of the judgment of Israel.

★Peter was anticipating the arrival of the world of righteousness foretold by the prophets (2 Peter 3.1-2; 13).

★Daniel 9 foretold the coming of the world of righteousness.

★Therefore, Peter was anticipating the coming of the world of righteousness foretold by Daniel.

If Peter was still anticipating the arrival of the world of righteousness foretold by Daniel (and Isaiah), then of necessity, that means the seventy weeks of Daniel 9 had not yet been fulfilled. Significantly, the contributors to *WSTTB*, completely ignore the connection between Daniel 9 and 2 Peter 3, in spite of the fact that Peter clearly said he was looking for the fulfillment of God's Old Covenant promises to Israel.

The world of righteousness foretold by Daniel would be fulfilled by the end of the seventy weeks of Daniel (Daniel 9.24). *There is no justification for saying the world of righteousness would arrive after the seventy weeks.* Thus, again, if the world of righteousness anticipated by Peter was the world of righteousness foretold by Daniel, this is *prima facie* proof that the seventy weeks of Daniel 9 were not fulfilled in AD 35.

And here is the application to the doctrine of resurrection.
The New Creation of 2 Peter 3 is the New Creation of Revelation 21-22.
The arrival of the New Creation of 2 Peter 3 and Revelation 21 is the time of the resurrection.
However, the arrival of the New Creation of 2 Peter 3 and Revelation 21-22 is the world of righteousness foretold by Daniel.
Since that New Creation is confined to the seventy weeks, this means the fulfillment of the resurrection world of righteousness of 2 Peter 3 and Revelation 21-22 is confined to the seventy weeks of Daniel 9.

The resurrection world of righteousness of 2 Peter 3 and Revelation 21-22 is confined to the seventy weeks of Daniel 9.

But the seventy weeks of Daniel 9 was fulfilled no later than the destruction of Jerusalem in AD 70.

Therefore, the resurrection world of righteousness of 2 Peter 3 and Revelation 21-22 was fulfilled no later than the destruction of Jerusalem in AD 70.

The only way to counter this argument is to prove the world of righteousness foretold by Daniel is not the world of righteousness foretold by Peter. But remember, in Acts 3, as Peter anticipated the "restoration of al things," which is indubitably the New Creation of 2 Peter 3, he said that anticipation time would be in fulfillment of all the prophets, from Moses,

Samuel, and all who had ever written. Thus, Peter's New Creation of 2 Peter 3 was in fact the New Creation promised in the Tanakh.

The authors of *WSTTB* simply take it for granted that Peter is speaking of "New Covenant" eschatology, without so much as a syllable of proof that Daniel is not the source for Peter's eschatology. Yet, Peter said his prophecy was taken from the Old Covenant prophecies. Where then are the Old Covenant prophecies of the destruction of literal heaven and earth followed by a literal new creation?

If the New Creation of Revelation is, as Gentry suggests, the full arrival of the promise made in Isaiah 65, then Revelation is the promise of the full arrival of the world of righteousness foretold by Daniel 9. These are parallel prophecies. But, if Revelation 21 anticipated the fulfillment of Isaiah 65 and Daniel 9 at AD 70, it most assuredly anticipated the resurrection at that time, for *the New Creation of Revelation 21 is the resurrection world of chapter 20.12f.*

Consider again the question of "How is this possible?" Futurists tell us Revelation 20-22 is to be fulfilled literally, at the end of the space-time universe. That will be followed by the establishment– the creation– of the New Heaven and Earth, as well as the New Jerusalem.

So, according to all of these futurist concepts, *supposedly shared by Hymenaeus,* we are supposed to believe Hymenaeus and his cohort were successfully convincing significant numbers of Christians into believing those events had already happened! Are we to seriously consider the idea that anyone could be so ignorant, so non-observant, so naive, as to believe the cosmos was destroyed yesterday, and YHVH had created a brand new material time space universe? We are supposed to believe Hymenaeus himself actually believed that event had already happened? The idea is absurd.

To Seal Up Vision and Prophecy

The fourth element of Daniel 9 is the promise that the seventy weeks were determined, "to seal up vision and prophecy." Mathison, probably following Mauro,[68] has a unique view of this term: "The eyes and ears of the Jews were 'sealed' from understanding the prophecies of God."(*Hope*, 221). There is no proof for this rather eccentric offering. This makes "vision and prophecy" refer to the people of Israel rather than the prophetic revelation and I know of no passage, or commentator, who has ever suggested that Israel (or their eyes and ears!), be identified as "vision and prophecy."

Gentry vacillates. He says the term means, "By this is meant that Christ fulfills (and thereby confirms) the prophecy (Luke 18.31; cf. Luke 24.44; Acts 3.18)." (*Dominion*, 316). However, in his monograph contra Gruden, commenting on "that which is perfect" of 1 Corinthians 13, he says, "there is coming a time when will occur the completion of the revelatory process of God."[69] He offers a footnote to that comment "We even believe that this idea is contained in a proper understanding of Daniel 9.24 statement regarding the "sealing of the vision and prophecy." (Ibid, N.4). So, on the one hand seal up vision and prophecy refers to Christ's atoning work and on the other hand it refers to the completion of the revelatory process.

Perhaps Gentry, "saw the train coming" after he wrote against Gruden. If he takes the position that "seal up vision and prophecy" is referent to the revelatory process, then, if he posits the completion of the seventy weeks in AD 35 (as he does), *the revelatory process must have been finished and sealed up through fulfillment by AD 35.*

So, it *seems* as if Gentry has retreated to the view that Daniel's prediction that vision and prophecy would be sealed by the end of the seventieth week is referent to the fulfillment of Daniel's prophecy of Christ's atoning work. This does not help.

---

[68] Philip Mauro, *The Seventy Weeks and the Great Tribulation,* (PA, Bible Truth Depot, I. C../ Herendeen, Swengel Union Co., 1944)50+.

[69] Kenneth Gentry, *The Charismatic Gift of Prophecy,* (Memphis, Tn., Footstool Publications, 1989)54.

As already seen, the putting away of sin and the atonement were not consummated at the cross. That process *included the resurrection* since the parousia is the consummation of atonement *to put away sin.*

Gentry tries to limit the definition and application of "vision and prophecy" to the prophecy of Daniel 9 instead of the prophetic corpus comprehensively considered. The reader will notice that he says seal up vison and prophecy refers to the fulfillment of *"the* prophecy" i.e. the prophecy of Daniel 9. This is unjustified. As I show in my work on Daniel 9, all scholars agree there is no definite article in the Hebrew to justify the rendering "seal up *the* vision and *the* prophecy."[70] The fact that there is no definite article in the Hebrew text means Gentry is not justified to claim the seventy weeks were determined to fulfill "the" prophecy of Daniel 9. Further, there is a widespread consensus, across all eschatological borders, that "seal up vision and prophecy" is a comprehensive term referring to the prophetic corpus as a whole (*Preston, Seal*, 1f).

With that said, we could actually allow Gentry's position that seventy weeks were determined to fulfill Daniel 9, since, properly understood, *Daniel 9 is a prophecy of the resurrection.* As we have shown, the putting away of sin and the making of the atonement are eschatological and soteriological ideas inextricably linked with resurrection. You cannot say the atonement was consummated at the Cross, because Hebrews 9 says it would be finished at the "Second Coming." But if the atonement was to be finished at the "Second Coming," that means *sin was to be put away* then and this is *resurrection.* Thus, since Daniel confines the putting away of sin and the making of atonement to the seventy weeks, it is possible for one to argue that seventy weeks were determined for the fulfillment of Daniel 9 and that would *still* posit resurrection at the end of the seventy weeks.

---

[70] In a public debate with Thomas Thrasher, March 13, 2004, I noted the absence of an article in the Hebrew text. Thrasher claimed, *contrary to all Hebrew scholars*, that the article is present. He did admit the article is "supplied." I had two with Thrasher and both are available from me.

The correlation between Daniel 9 and the Olivet Discourse must be examined. Daniel was told seventy weeks were determined to "seal up vision and prophecy." This means the confirmation through fulfillment, of all vision and prophecy. Jesus agreed that all prophecy would be fulfilled in the fall of Jerusalem. In Luke 21.22 Jesus spoke of the catastrophe to come on Jerusalem: "These be the days of vengeance in which all things that are written must be fulfilled."[71]

Now, how much of "vision and prophecy" would be left out of the fulfillment of "all things that are written"? Remember, Jesus in Luke is describing his coming, the coming *to finish the atonement* (Hebrews 9.28; 10.35-38), that is confined to the seventy weeks. But, that coming and that atoning work, is to "seal up vision and prophecy." Thus, Daniel, and Jesus drawing from Daniel, posited the fulfillment of the entire prophetic corpus at the time of the fall of Jerusalem in AD 70. That means that the resurrection had to occur by or at that time.

Jesus earlier posited the fulfillment of all prophecy, "Verily I say unto you, until heaven and earth passes away, not one jot, nor one tittle shall pass from the Law, until it is all fulfilled" (Matthew 5.17-18). Notice that Jesus placed the passing of "heaven and earth" at the time of the fulfillment of all things in "the law and the prophets." And what do we find in the Olivet Discourse? We find the passing of "heaven and earth" (Matthew 24.29f, the Old Covenant world of Israel),[72] at the time when "all things that are

---

[71] Gentry confidently claims he has found a fatal flaw in the true preterist appeal to Luke 21.22. He says the "naive" hermeneutic of preterists overlooks the Greek tenses of the text and says the force of Luke 21.22 is simply that all prophecy that had been given prior to the fall of Jerusalem and that dealt with that event, were the focus of Jesus' words. Gentry failed to realize that his own words are fatal to his Postmillennialism, as I noted in my response to his article. You can see his article and my response on my website:
http://eschatology.org/index.php?option=com_content&view=article&id=678:kenneth-gentrys-latest-desperation&catid=73:engaging-the-critics&Itemid=211.

[72] Gentry, Jordan, Mathison, DeMar, and most partial preterists agree that the "heaven and earth" of Old Covenant

written must be fulfilled." Are we supposed to ignore the perfect correlation between Daniel, Matthew 5.17-18 and the Olivet Discourse? Daniel was told the end of the seventy weeks would see the fulfillment of vision and prophecy and the end of that vision would be the fall of Jerusalem. Jesus said none of the Old Law could pass until heaven and earth passed at the fulfillment of every jot and tittle of the Law. And in the Olivet Discourse, Jesus said "all things that are written" would be fulfilled at the destruction of the temple and Jerusalem, Israel's "heaven and earth."[73]

Jesus said not one jot or tittle of the Law would pass until it was all fulfilled. Resurrection was part of "the law" (Acts 24.14-15). Daniel said "vision and prophecy" the entire prophetic corpus, would be fulfilled by the end of the seventy weeks. The end of the seventy weeks was no later than AD 70. Therefore, the resurrection was fulfilled no later than AD 70.

So, what have we seen in this section? We have seen that the term "seal up vision and prophecy" refers to the comprehensive fulfillment of the entire prophetic corpus. That would be accomplished by the end of the seventy weeks.

We have seen that attempts like those of Gentry, Mathison, etc., to limit the application of "seal up vision and prophecy" to just the prophecy of Daniel 9 specifically, backfire. *Daniel 9 is actually a prediction of the resurrection.* Even if, therefore, one successfully argued that "seal up vision and prophecy" actually meant "seal up *the* vision and *the* prophecy" of Daniel 9, it would still mean that within the seventy weeks, the resurrection would take place.

Israel passed away in the destruction of Jerusalem.

[73] The Jerusalem temple was called "heaven and earth" by the Jews of Jesus' day. Josephus, Ant. 3:6:4 and 3:7:7 says the Jews called the temple, with its Holy and Most Holy Place, "heaven and earth." Thus, as Jesus predicted the destruction of the temple, it was perfectly natural for him to say "heaven and earth will pass away" (Matthew 24.35). He was not speaking of the material cosmos. He was speaking of the Jewish "heaven and earth."

We have seen that attempts to short circuit the application of "seal up vision and prophecy" to only a few events within the seventy weeks, while the majority of application falls outside the divinely decreed Heptads, are misguided.

We have seen the perfect correlation between Daniel and Jesus' predictions about when all prophecy would be fulfilled, at the end of the Old Covenant age of Israel in AD 70.

What we have seen therefore, is that Daniel 9.24f foretold the resurrection, because it foretold the time of the putting away of sin, the atonement, the everlasting world of righteousness and the fulfillment of all prophecy. And all of that was to be accomplished *within*, not outside, the seventy weeks that terminated in the fall of Jerusalem in AD 70.

In light of the above points, it should be more than evident why the modern charge of the Hymenaean Heresy against preterists is fundamentally wrong. Those making the charge are themselves ignoring the undeniable framework for the resurrection given repeatedly in the Tanakh. As we have seen, this is precisely what every one of the contributors to *WSTTB* do. It is as if Daniel had no connection to the resurrection. They completely ignore the indisputable fact that the framework for the resurrection is the time of the judgment of Jerusalem in AD 70.

POINT #5
RESURRECTION: THE HOPE OF *ISRAEL*!

One of the greatest shortcomings of futurist eschatology is the failure to see that Biblically, eschatology is related to the promises to Israel, not the end of time or the Christian age. We shall see how this applies specifically to the charge of the Hymenaean Heresy below. For now, we want to demonstrate that resurrection was indeed "the hope of Israel," and how Biblical truth is being distorted or ignored.

A prime example of this distortion is *WSTTB*. [74] As we have seen, the book purports to be a definitive refutation of Covenant Eschatology and has chapters by Kenneth Gentry, Charles Hill, Richard Pratt, Douglas Wilson and Simon Kistemaker. Each of the contributors to *WSTTB*, whether Postmillennial or Amillennial, believe eschatology is linked to *the end of the Christian age* and the termination of "human history." In reality, Biblical eschatology has *nothing* to do with the end of the Christian age. It has nothing to do with the end of time. It has nothing to do with the end of human history. Biblical eschatology is *Covenant Eschatology*, not Historical Eschatology.

As Paul was on trial, he said his doctrine of the resurrection was foretold in "the law" and "Moses and the prophets" (Acts 24.14f). Before Agrippa, he said he was on trial, "for the hope of the promise made to our fathers." That hope was resurrection, for which "our twelve tribes, earnestly serving God night and day, hope to attain" (Acts 26.6f). He preached that hope *as the gospel* and, it was, again, from Moses and the prophets (26.22f).

In Romans 8, the apostle wrote some of his more eloquent words in anticipation of, "the adoption, to wit, the redemption of the body" (Romans 8.23). This is, of course, resurrection. What is so often ignored or overlooked is that the promise of the adoption belonged to Israel "after the flesh" (Romans 9.3-5) and was not a promise given to the church divorced

---

[74] As already noted, see the response to this book, *House Divided: A Reformed Response to When Shall These Things Be*. David Green, Edward Hassert and Michael Sullivan contributors. (Vision Press, Ramona, Ca. 2012). This book is available from my websites.

from Israel. Likewise, in 1 Corinthians 15, Paul was looking for the fulfillment of God's OT resurrection promises to Israel (1 Corinthians 15.54) for he says the resurrection would be when Isaiah 25 and Hosea 13 would be fulfilled.

It is an egregious distortion of the text to make Isaiah 25 and Hosea 13 refer to the raising of physical bodies out of the ground. Both texts, and virtually all OT resurrection prophecies, predicted the salvation from "sin-death," i.e. alienation from God caused by sin.

The point is, when the NT writers foretold the resurrection, they were Jews *anticipating the fulfillment of God's promises to Israel* by the power of Messiah Jesus (cf. Acts 3.19f). They were not preaching a replacement theology that said Israel was not going to be given her promises as a result of her sin. They were not saying Israel had failed and so, her promises were now given to the church. They were not, as claimed by Pratt above, saying the end times had been postponed, due to Jewish unbelief. They were saying that what was happening, and what was about to happen, was the fulfillment of what was actually foretold.[75] God was faithful to His promises (Romans 11.29f). Thus, the resurrection promises made to Israel had not been taken from her and transferred to the church to be fulfilled at the end of the church age. Israel's promises were to be fulfilled in *her last days*, at the climax of *her history*, at the Day of the Lord.

Daniel 9.24-27 is the prediction of the consummation of Israel's soteriological and eschatological hope. The removal of Israel's sins is inextricably linked with the parousia of Jesus in fulfillment of "all that the prophets have spoken" (Acts 3.21f): "repent so that your sins may be blotted out...and that He may send Jesus."

---

[75] See Mark Nanos, *The Mystery of Romans*, (Minneapolis, Fortress, 1996). Nanos rightfully shows how Paul's message to Israel was one of *fulfillment*. Even his Gentile mission was in *fulfillment of God's promises to Israel*, not an indication of failure. While there are issues in Nanos we would reject, he nonetheless does a good job establishing this premise.

God's covenant with Israel would be fulfilled, "when I take away their sins," *at the parousia of Jesus* (Romans 11.26-27). One does not have to wonder where Paul got the idea of the removal of Israel's sin. Daniel promised: "Seventy weeks are determined...to put away sin...to make atonement for iniquity."[76]

The promise of the New Heavens and Earth, the world of everlasting righteousness, was promised, not to the church at the end of the church age, but it was *Israel's hope* (2 Peter 3.1-2; Revelation 21-22.6).

> **To divorce Biblical eschatology from Israel and transfer it to the end of the church age is to completely distort the Biblical evidence. Eschatology belongs to the last days of Israel, not the last days of time or the Christian age.**

When we read 1 Thessalonians 4.13f we are reading about God's promise to Israel. When we read 2 Thessalonians 1, we are reading about the fulfillment of God's promises to Israel.[77] When we read Acts, Romans, 2 Peter 3, or Revelation, *we are reading about God's faithfulness to His promises to Israel.* To posit New Testament eschatological promises outside the framework and the time of God's judgment of Israel is to do a grave disservice to Biblical exegesis and hermeneutic.

---

[76] See also Romans 11.25-27 that alludes to three OT prophecies, Jeremiah 31; Isaiah 27 and Isaiah 59. The common theme in the two Isaianic prophecies is that Israel would be saved through judgment. This is what Daniel foretold.

[77] See my discussion of 2 Thessalonians 1 in my book, *In Flaming Fire*. Paul quotes directly from Isaiah 2.10; 19-21 in his prediction of the Day of the Lord. Isaiah 2-4 is a prediction of the last days when Israel would be judged for her blood guilt (4.4; cf. Matthew 23), when her men would die by the edge of the sword (3.18-24). Jesus applied those identical verses from Isaiah to his judgment coming against Jerusalem. If Jesus applied Isaiah to Israel's judgment in AD 70, what right does anyone have to apply Paul's use of those verses to the end of church history?

We offer the following for consideration:

> The resurrection, the parousia of Christ and the New Creation promises were the salvation hope of Israel.
>
> But, the salvation hope of Israel would be fulfilled by the end of the seventy weeks of Daniel 9.
>
> Therefore, the resurrection, the parousia of Christ and the New Creation promises to Israel would be fulfilled by the end of the seventy weeks of Daniel 9.

And following that, we offer this:

> The resurrection, the parousia of Christ and the New Creation promises to Israel would be fulfilled by the end of the seventy weeks of Daniel 9.
>
> But, the seventy weeks of Daniel 9 were fulfilled no later than AD 70.
>
> Therefore, the resurrection, the parousia of Christ and the New Creation promises to Israel were fulfilled no later than AD 70.

Futurists say the resurrection is at the end of the Christian age.

Hymenaeus said the resurrection was already past.

We are supposed to believe Hymenaeus was saying the (endless!!) Christian age– all of 30+ years old– had come to an end?

How can anyone seriously make such a claim?

With this in mind, consider again how ludicrous the charge of the Hymenaean Heresy is. Futurists insist the resurrection occurs *at the end of the Christian age*. Hymenaeus supposedly believed the same thing, per the futurist "argument." Yet, Hymenaeus said the resurrection had already passed. Let's look at a couple of possibilities:

Hymenaeus knew the resurrection belonged to the end of the Old Covenant age of Israel, in fulfillment of her promises.

Or,

He believed the resurrection belongs to the end of the Christian age, in fulfillment of either New Promises, or, Israel's promises, stolen from her and transferred to the church.

Now, if Hymenaeus knew and believed the resurrection belonged to the end of the Old Covenant age of Israel, and he said it was past, then futurists have a severe problem. Why is that? Because futurists almost all insist that Israel's covenant age had already ended. It ended at the cross. But, this gets very troublesome, very quickly, for the futurists.

Almost all futurists claim the Law of Moses was removed at the cross. Well, the resurrection promises made to Israel were found in "Moses, the law and the prophets" (Acts 3.19f; 24.14f). So, if "Moses, the Law and the prophets" was removed at the cross, then since it could not pass until it was all, every jot and every tittle, fulfilled, then of necessity, "Moses, the Law and the prophets" *inclusive of the resurrection promises*, was fulfilled at the cross.

This means that Paul -- who *supposedly* taught that the Law of Moses passed at the cross[78] -- was confused when he denied the fulfillment and passing of the Law at the cross in 2 Timothy 2.17f *by denying the fulfillment of the OT resurrection promises.* Since the resurrection is, as we demonstrate in this work, tied inextricably to the end of Israel's covenant age, if the Old Covenant passed at the cross, the resurrection had to have been fulfilled when Paul condemned Hymenaeus! Was Paul that confused? How could Paul affirm the passing of Torah and yet, deny that the resurrection was past?

The only other choice here is that Hymenaeus believed – as futurists today do– the resurrection comes at the end of the Christian age. But, are we

---

[78] See my *From Torah To Telos: The Passing of the Law of Moses*, (Vol. I).

supposed to believe Hymenaeus was saying the (endless!!) New Covenant age of Christ– which was only approximately 30+ years old -- had already come to an end? In light of the fact that both the Old Covenant and the New teach that the New Covenant world would never end, never pass away (Matthew 24.35) never be removed (Hebrews 12.26-28) how in the world could Hymenaeus teach such a thing? Biblically, the only age that was to end was the imperfect, intrinsically temporary, Mosaic Covenant age. It was the age tied to the temple in Jerusalem (Matthew 24.1-3): The age of Moses and the Law.

DANIEL 9 AND DANIEL 12

Partial preterists such as Gentry, McDurmon, Mathison, etc. have no problem teaching that Daniel 9 extends no further than AD 70. As we have seen, most Dominionists of the day posit the end of the seventieth week well before AD 70. However, they normally deny– or fail to see -- that Daniel 9 is a promise of the resurrection. While many deny Daniel 9 predicts the resurrection, they affirm that Daniel 12 does predict the "final" resurrection. Thus, if Daniel 9 and Daniel 12 are parallel passages this would demonstrate the fulfillment of the resurrection by AD 70. The following chart will prove that the passages are parallel.

DANIEL 9	DANIEL 12
Concerning Israel (V. 24)	Concerning Israel (V. 1-7)
Time of the end (V. 27)	Time of the end (V. 4)
Abomination of Desolation (V. 27)	Abomination of Desolation (V. 9F— cf. Matthew 24.15)
Resurrection (Atonement)[79]	Resurrection (V. 2)
Fulfilled by AD 70	"When power of the holy people is shattered." (V. 7)

Patently, Daniel 9 and Daniel 12 are parallel passages. This is significant because Strimple, Hill and Mathison all cite Daniel 12 as predictive of the "final resurrection" at the end of human history. This presents a dilemma for the authors of *WSTTB*.

Daniel 9 and 12 are prophecies about the consummation of God's Covenant dealings with Israel. These passages are not about the end of time. They are not about the end of the Christian age. Mathison and most other partial preterists would concur with the true preterists that at least Daniel 9 has

---

[79] The Atonement -- just as the putting away of sin -- is linked to the second coming. The second coming is at the resurrection, therefore, the Atonement is tied to the resurrection.

nothing to do with the end of the Christian age. But, if Daniel 9 has nothing to do with the church age, neither does Daniel 12.

Daniel 12 is the prediction of the "final resurrection" at the end of human history[80] (Mathison, Hill, Strimple and virtually all partial preterists). But, Daniel 12 is parallel, (speaks of the same time and same events) with Daniel 9.24-27). Therefore, Daniel 9 is the prediction of the "final resurrection" at the end of human history. Do partial preterists believe Daniel 9 speaks of the end of human history? No. Do partial preterists believe Daniel 9 even speaks of the "final resurrection?" No, not generally. Yet, it is abundantly clear that Daniel 9 and Daniel 12 do predict the same time and same events.

Daniel 9 and Daniel 12 are parallel passages, speaking of the same time and same events. But, the events of Daniel 9 were all were confined to the seventy weeks that ended no later than the time of the fall of Jerusalem in AD 70. Therefore, the events of Daniel 12 were all confined to a period of time no later than the fall of Jerusalem in AD 70. But, if the events of Daniel 12 were confined to a period of time no later than AD 70, this means that the resurrection of the dead was confined to a period of time no later than AD 70. Daniel was told this exact thing.

Notice that Daniel 12.2 predicted the resurrection. Verse 3 is the prediction of the time of the end when the righteous would shine as the sun. Jesus said this text would be fulfilled at the time of his coming at the end of the age (Matthew 13.43). As a rule, partial preterists apply Matthew 13 to the end of the church age.[81]

---

[80] See my *AD 70: A Shadow of the "Real" End?*

[81] See my discussion of Matthew 13 and Daniel 12 in my *Babylon* book.

Daniel 12.4 instructed Daniel to seal up his book "until the time of the end" (*heos kairou sunteleias*).[82] It was far removed from his day, reserved for the "end."

Thus, in Daniel 12.2-4 we have two major eschatological passages. The prediction of the resurrection and the prediction of the time of the end, that Jesus applied to the end of the age, the time of the harvest.

In verses 5-7, Daniel overheard one angel ask another: "How long shall the fulfillment of these wonders be?" Undeniably, the question involves the time of the end and the resurrection. Heaven's answer is given as one angel raised his hands to heaven and swore by the name of Jehovah: "when the power of the holy people has been completely shattered, all these things shall be finished."

Mathison says Daniel 12.5-7 is one of several passages giving "nonspecific time frames" for its eschatological predictions (*WSTTB*, 164). Now, while Daniel 12.7 does not give "the day or the hour" for the time of the resurrection and time of the end, the marker it does give is unmistakable and undeniable: "when the power of the holy people is completely shattered, all these things will be finished." Mathison is simply obfuscating.

Can there be any doubt as to when the power of the holy people was completely shattered? The holy people here cannot be the church being destroyed at the end of the Christian age. The kingdom will never be destroyed (Daniel 2.44; 7.13f). Further, there is no place in the Postmillennial or Amillennial paradigm for a total destruction of Israel at the end of the Christian age. Both views believe Israel was finally

---

[82] There is virtual unanimity among the scholars that the LXX Greek term "time of the end" from Daniel 12.4 is the source for the references to the time of the end in Matthew 13.39f and Matthew 24. Jesus and the disciples clearly had Daniel's prediction of the end in mind in their discussions of the end.

destroyed in AD 70.[83] This being true, this demands the resurrection of Daniel 12 was fulfilled in AD 70.

Of course this agrees perfectly with Daniel 9. The time of the resurrection is the time of the putting away of sin, *the making of the atonement* and the time of the fulfillment of all things as we have seen. So, the time of the making of the atonement of Daniel 9 is the time of the resurrection of Daniel 12. But, the making of the atonement of Daniel 9 is confined to and would be fulfilled no later than AD 70. Therefore, the time of the resurrection of Daniel 12.2 is confined to and would be fulfilled no later than AD 70.

It cannot be argued that Daniel 12 foretold some kind of spiritual resurrection that occurred in AD 70, which then foreshadowed and typified the "real" resurrection at the end of time. If Daniel 12.2 is a prediction of the "final resurrection" as Hill, Mathison, Strimple and Gentry affirm, it is not a prophecy of AD 70 at all. And to my knowledge, none of these men have affirmed this in *WSTTB*. They offer Daniel 12 as a straightforward prediction of the end, not a shadow, not a type,[84] but of the "real" resurrection.[85] So, again, if Daniel 12.2 is predictive of the "final

---

[83] Classical Postmillennialism certainly has no place for a future total destruction of "the power of the holy people" since it posits the conversion of the majority of Israel at the end of the millennium.

[84] It is, however, increasingly common for Dominionists and Amillennialists to claim AD 70 did foreshadow the "real end." I address that claim in my *AD 70: A Shadow of the "Real" End?*

[85] Of course, in one of the most lamentable chapters of *WSTTB*, Pratt argues that "even if the scriptures did predict Jesus' return would take place within a few years, his return could still be in our future, even two thousand years later" (*WSTTB*, 2004, 122). For Pratt, God's prophetic word is totally contingent on man's response. Thus, precisely like the Millennialists, Pratt argues that although God may have given a time for the fulfillment of His Word, that does not mean anything! God can postpone His promises, indefinitely it

resurrection" as the partial preterists affirm, there can be no doubt about when the resurrection was to occur. It was, "when the power of the holy people" was completely shattered. And that was at the end of the Old Covenant world of Israel in AD 70.

---

would seem, and that does not affect our view of His faithfulness or His Sovereignty. Pratt has surrendered any valid objection to the millennial gap (postponement) theory and one can only wonder how Mathison, Gentry, DeMar, etc. will react. These men are normally opposed to the millennial gap theory and yet, Mathison has, by including Pratt's chapter, posited that as a valid response to preterism.

POINT #6
ROMANS 11, DANIEL 9,
AND THE END OF ISRAEL'S HISTORY

To extrapolate Romans 11 beyond the first century framework is unjustified and violates the demands of the text. As we have just seen, Romans gives no justification for a future salvation of Israel. Romans 11 was fulfilled at the end of the seventy weeks of Daniel 9.

Romans 11.25-27 would be fulfilled when God's covenant dealings with Israel were consummated. The time of the salvation of Israel is posited as the time "when I take away their sins" (v. 27). When does Daniel say Israel's sin would be removed? *Within the* seventy *weeks.* The question is, upon what basis does one delineate between the taking away of Israel's sin in Romans and the putting away of sin in Daniel? Is the prophecy of Daniel different than the prophecies underlying Romans, i.e. Isaiah 27 and Isaiah 59? If the promise of Romans is the same promise of Isaiah and Daniel, then since the promise of Daniel is confined to the seventy weeks, this means the parousia of Christ promised in Romans is confined to the seventy weeks -- and this destroys the partial preterist construct.

This point can hardly be over-emphasized. Remember that the putting away of the sin of Israel belongs to the seventy weeks of Daniel 9. Most Postmillennialists, Gentry, DeMar, Mathison, et. al. believe the seventy weeks were fulfilled circa 34-35. Yet, Gentry and Mathison, as well as traditional Postmillennialists, believe Romans 11.25f refers to a yet future conversion of Israel. However, this simply will not work.

Daniel 9 foretold the same putting away of sin anticipated by Paul in Romans 11.Therefore, Romans 11 is confined to the seventy weeks of Daniel 9. However, since Paul was still anticipating the fulfillment of that prophecy, the putting away of Israel's sins of Daniel 9, when he wrote circa AD 57, the seventy weeks of Daniel 9 were not fulfilled and terminated circa AD 34-35.

This has devastating consequences for the Postmillennial view, for it is held that the conversion of the Jews comes near or at *the end of the millennium,* i.e. just before the "final" coming of the Lord.[86] So, if Paul was anticipating the fulfillment of Daniel's prophecy and if, as Postmillennialists affirm, the conversion of Israel occurs near the end of the millennium, it therefore follows that Paul believed the end of the millennium was near when he wrote.

Unless the Postmillennialists are willing to extrapolate the seventieth week of Daniel 9 into the still distant future–thus allowing for a still future fulfillment of the putting away of sin[87] -- we must confine the fulfillment

---

[86] Tremendous changes are taking place within Postmillennialism. Many of the long held, creedally stated views on major eschatological verses are being rejected by modern Dominionists such as Gentry, DeMar, McDurmon, etc. The long held Postmillennial view on Romans 11.25f is one example of the dramatic changes being made. The creedal view is that Paul foretold a yet future conversion of the nation of Israel at the end of the Christian age. But some of these men now say Romans 11 was actually fulfilled no later than AD 70, rejecting the classic Postmillennial view of Romans 11.25f. Joel McDurmon, *Jesus V Jerusalem*, (Powder Springs, Ga., American Vision, 2011)220, commenting on Romans 11, rejects the Westminster Confession of faith. He says he finds the views in the Larger Catechism "unconvincing." McDurmon's inconsistency is, however, revealed in the fact that prior to our July 2012 formal debate, he said God's covenant with Israel will remain valid until the "physical resurrection." If God's covenant with Israel remains intact until the end of human history, Romans 11 has not been fulfilled. Paul undeniably posits the parousia of Romans 11 as the climax of Israel's covenant history.

[87] To do this of course, the Postmillennialists would be creating the exact same "gap" between the sixty ninth and the seventieth week of Daniel 9 that they so decry in the millennial construct. If the putting away of sin of Daniel 9 and the putting away of sin in Romans are the same, then patently, if the fulfillment of the seventieth week is still future, the seventieth week was postponed just as the Millennialists say. There is no justification for delineating between the putting away of sin in these two texts. Therefore, unless the

of that final consummative week to the first century context. But, if the fulfillment of that final week occurred in the first century, at Christ's parousia in AD 70, it therefore strips the Postmillennialists of one of their most important proof texts for a futurist eschatology.

Here is a series of arguments based on Daniel 9 and Romans as they relate to the consummation of Israel's history.

#1
The consummation of Old Covenant Israel's history would be the resurrection of the dead (Acts 24.14f; 26.6f / Romans 8.23; 9.3-5/ 1 Corinthians 15).

But, the consummation of Israel's history is confined to the seventy weeks of Daniel 9.24-27.

Therefore, the resurrection of the dead is confined to the seventy weeks of Daniel 9.24-27.

#2
The consummation of Israel's history would occur at the time of the parousia of Romans 11.

But, the parousia of Romans 11.25f occurred at the time of the judgment of Israel in AD 70 (Matthew 23 and the avenging of the martyrs).

Therefore, the consummation of Israel's history -- the resurrection -- occurred at the time of the judgment of Israel in AD 70

Postmillennialists are willing now to join the Millennialists in positing a gap between the sixty ninth and the seventieth week, they must cede Romans 11 to the first century, AD 70 parousia of Christ, thus stripping their eschatology of one of their most fundamental arguments for futurism. And of course, as we have noted in this work, that is precisely what is happening among some Dominionists.

#3
The consummation of Israel's history – when God's promises to her would be fulfilled -- would be when sin was "put away" (Daniel 9.24).

But the time when God fulfilled His promises to Israel by putting away sin would be at the parousia of Romans 11.25-27.

Therefore, the parousia of Romans 11.25-27 would be the consummation of Israel's history.

#4
The parousia of Romans 11.25-27 would be the consummation of Israel's history.

But, the consummation of Israel's history would be the resurrection of the dead (Acts 24.4f; 26.6f/ Romans 8.23; 9.3f / 1 Corinthians 15).

Therefore, the parousia of Romans 11.25-27 would be the resurrection of the dead (Notice Romans 11.15 where Paul affirms this very thing).

#5
The parousia of Romans 11.25-27 would be the resurrection of the dead

But, the parousia of Romans 11.25-27 was in AD 70.

Therefore, the resurrection of the dead was in AD 70.

#6
The consummation of Israel's history occurred at the time of the judgment of Israel in AD 70 (Daniel 9.24-27).

But the consummation of Israel's history would be the resurrection.

Therefore, the resurrection, at the consummation of Israel's history, occurred at the time of the judgment of Israel in AD 70.

#7
The consummation of Israel's history would be the resurrection (Acts 24-28/ Romans 8.23/ 1 Cor. 15).

The consummation of Israel's history is confined to the seventy weeks of Daniel 9.

The seventy weeks of Daniel 9 ended no later than AD 70.

Therefore, the consummation of Israel's history – *the resurrection* – is confined to the seventy weeks of Daniel 9 that ended no later than AD 70.

Paul was anticipating the consummation of God's promises to Israel. Furthermore, it is undeniable that Daniel 9 is concerned with the consummation of Israel's Messianic and soteriological hopes. So, if Daniel 9 and Romans 11 speak of the same time and same events, then since Daniel 9 de-limited the fulfillment of Israel's hope to the seventy weeks, it therefore follows, inexorably, that Romans 11.25-27 is confined to the seventy weeks of Daniel 9.

If Romans 11.25-27 is confined to the seventy weeks of Daniel 9, as demonstrated above, this means the parousia of Romans 11 is confined to the seventy weeks.[88] This also means if one posits the salvation of Israel for the last days of the millennium,[89] as do the Postmillennialists, it is

---

[88] The claim of many commentators that the coming of the Lord in Romans 11 was referent to Jesus' Incarnation is untenable. Riddlebarger says: "Paul, therefore, probably understands the future tenses of the Isaiah prophecy as fulfilled in the first coming of Christ, which set in motion the apostolic mission of the church." (Kim Riddlebarger, *Amillennialism*, (Grand Rapids, Baker, 2003)94. This view ignores the judgment context of Isaiah 27 / 59 from Paul which draws his hope for the salvation of Israel. Per Isaiah, Israel's salvation would come at the time of her judgment. Riddlebarger ignores this.

[89] In my debate with Jim Jordan, October 2004, Tampa, Florida, I gave a sampling of the evidence that can be produced in demonstration of this thesis. While all futurist eschatologies say we are either now in the millennium, or the millennium is yet future, the Bible shows, in no uncertain terms, that the millennium was in fact near its end in the first century, and ended in AD 70. Audio and video as well as a

irrefutably true that the end of the millennium was at the parousia of AD 70.

The only way to avoid this devastating impact on the Postmillennial paradigm[90] is:

a. to prove that the putting away of sin in Daniel 9 and in Romans 11 are different events at different times.

b. prove that Israel had, or has, two consummative, soteriological events. Yet, at least some of the leading Postmillennialists acknowledge that AD 70 was a redemptive-historical event of unparalleled importance.

c. to prove that perhaps the seventieth week of Daniel 9 has not yet been fulfilled. Of course to do this, one has to abandon the normal Postmillennial view that the seventieth week was fulfilled in AD 34-35. This would likewise be contra the Amillennial view of the seventy weeks. I am unaware of any Amillennial or Postmillennial commentator who extrapolates Daniel's seventieth week into the future.

Furthermore, to posit the seventieth week as yet future, inserts a 2000 year gap between the sixty-ninth and the seventieth week, something that both Postmillennialists and Amillennialists are normally loathe to do.

The fact is Daniel 9 and Romans 11 do speak of the same theme, the salvation of Israel. The two passages did foretell the same events and the same time. That being so, Romans 11 cannot be used to justify a yet future conversion of the Jews at the end of the current Christian age. Romans 11

---

book of the debate with Jordan are available from us. See Joseph Vincent's excellent book: *The Millennium: Past, Present or Future?* for a defense of the forty year millennial period.

[90] Naturally, it is not just the Postmillennial eschatology destroyed by the truth that the millennium ended circa AD 70. If the millennium ended circa AD 70, *all futurist eschatologies are falsified.*

anticipated the consummation of Israel's soteriological and eschatological history in AD 70.

Why is the question of the consummation of Israel's history so important? It is because *the resurrection is the consummation of Israel's history.*

Contra the normal belief that the resurrection is to be the fulfillment of eschatological promises made to the church, for the end of the Christian age, Paul said, *repeatedly*, his gospel was the "hope of Israel" and the core of the message was the resurrection (Acts 24.4f; 26; 6f; 26.23f; 28.20f). When the apostle wrote his greatest discourse on the resurrection he emphatically stated that the resurrection would be when the Old Covenant promises to Israel were fulfilled (1 Corinthians 15.54f). Thus, to repeat, the question about the consummation of Israel's history is the fundamental question of the resurrection. And of course, this is at the heart of the Hymenaean Heresy charge.

Daniel 9 and Romans 11 anticipated the consummation of Israel's history; this is undeniably true. Since Daniel 9 posited the consummation of Israel's history at the destruction of Jerusalem in AD 70, this is the time of the resurrection.

We have demonstrated how the partial preterists agree that Daniel 9 cannot extend beyond the first century.

We have shown, and the partial preterists agree, Daniel 9 is not concerned with the church, or the church age, *per se*, but with the consummation of the hopes of Israel.

We have shown that the seventy weeks of Daniel 9 did not end before AD 70 and they cannot extend into our future.

We have shown how the partial preterists stop short of the correct application of the promises of Daniel 9. The putting away of sin, the atonement, the bringing in of everlasting righteousness and the fulfillment of vision and prophecy were not consummated at the Cross.

We have shown that the putting away of sin, the atonement, the bringing in of everlasting righteousness and the sealing up of vision and prophecy are all inextricably related to the "final resurrection."

We have shown that each of the constituent elements promised in Daniel are related to the resurrection of the dead. This means the seventy weeks of Daniel cannot be extended further than the destruction of Jerusalem in AD 70. It means the "final resurrection" must have occurred at the time of the fall of Jerusalem in AD 70.

We have demonstrated that Daniel 9 and Daniel 12 are parallel passages that were fulfilled at the end of the Old Covenant age of Israel in AD 70. And, since Daniel 12.2 predicted the resurrection, this means the resurrection of Daniel 12.2 was fulfilled, "when the power of the holy people" was "completely shattered."

We have proven that all attempts to posit a future for ethnic Israel, at a future parousia of Christ, violates the text of Romans 11. Romans 11 had to be fulfilled within the same parameters as Daniel 9, the seventy weeks.

We have proven that Romans 11 and Daniel 9 predicted the same time and same event, the consummation of the history/hope of Israel.

We have shown that the consummation of Israel's hope was the resurrection. Since therefore, the consummation of Daniel 9 was to be in AD 70 and Daniel 9 and Romans 11 are prophetically synchronous events in regard to fulfillment, it follows that the resurrection in fulfillment of Israel's history and hope was in AD 70.

Daniel 9 therefore, is normative in defining the framework and the time for the resurrection of the dead. Daniel 9 demands that the resurrection of the dead occurred at the end of the Old Covenant age of Israel in AD 70.

We have presented a good bit of strong evidence for our argumentation, and demonstrated the weakness in the argumentation and logic of those who condemn the true preterist view. How does all of this impact our study of the Hymenaean Heresy? It shows that those who try to use 2 Timothy 2 to condemn preterists are using an anachronistic hermeneutic. *Hymenaeus was making his claims prior to the time of the resurrection* and was therefore, clearly wrong. On the other hand, you and I live after the time determined by God for the resurrection.

To call a person a heretic based on 2 Timothy 2 ignores the fact that God said the resurrection was to occur at the end of the Old Covenant age of Israel.

To call a person a heretic based on 2 Timothy 2 ignores the fact that resurrection belonged to Israel.

To call a person a heretic based on 2 Timothy 2 and claim the resurrection is still future, is to create a totally new, biblically unknown eschaton. It is to suggest that the unending Christian age will after all, have an end. This is a clear violation of inspiration.

To properly use 2 Timothy 2 as a basis for charging anyone with heresy, one must prove (or accept) that Israel remains God's chosen people and Israel's Old Covenant promises are yet valid. Oh, wait, that would not work, would it? It still would not explain how Hymenaeus could say the end of human history had already happened.

Furthermore, to prove that Israel's eschatological promises are still valid would invalidate Amillennialism and call Postmillennialism into question as well. This is illustrated by Riddlebarger's view of the Old Covenant: "Because of Jesus Christ and his coming, the Christian possesses the complete fulfillment and blessings of all the promises of the messianic age made under the old covenant. But, the arrival of the messianic age also brought with it a new series of promises to be fulfilled at the end of the age. The fulfilled promises pointed to a more glorious and future fulfillment. This is called the 'not yet' or future eschatology. It is this already/not yet tension which serves as the basis for understanding much of the New Testament eschatological expectation" (2003, 6).

Riddlebarger clearly fails to see that the promise of the resurrection belonged to Israel "after the flesh" (Romans 9.1-3) and it belonged to the consummation of her age, not a supposed "end of time."

They must be able to prove– *and admit* -- that the entirety of the Old Law remains valid.

They must be able to prove Israel's last days are yet future.[91]

Strangely, the majority of those who appeal to 2 Timothy 2 to charge preterists with heresy, do not believe *any* of these doctrines! It is therefore inherently self-contradictory for the Amillennialists and the Postmillennialists especially to utilize 2 Timothy 2 against advocates of Covenant Eschatology.

In short, to appeal to 2 Timothy 2 as a basis to charge preterists with heresy is not only misguided and inappropriate, it is simply *wrong*.

---

[91] As noted above, prior to my formal debate with Joel McDurmon, I asked him: "At what point of time and with what events were, or will, all of God's Old Covenant promises, made to Old Covenant Israel, be fulfilled and His covenant relationship with them terminated?" He responded that this will be at the physical resurrection. So, per McDurmon, God's covenant with Israel, *which was the Mosaic Covenant*, remains valid. Needless to say, this necessitates the abiding validity of all of Torah, not just some of it as held by McDurmon. This was a telling point in that debate. To add to the irony, McDurmon also tried to divorce the prophecies of the resurrection in Isaiah and Hosea, from the resurrection promise of Genesis 3 and Job. He also claimed that the eschatological promises to Abraham were not the eschatological promises to Israel.

When Amillennialists and Postmillennialists (especially) appeal to 2 Timothy 2 to condemn preterists, they are in fact revealing their own ignorance– or rejection– of the true source of New Testament eschatology.

All New Testament eschatology is the reiteration of God's Old Covenant promises made to Israel "after the flesh."

Any eschatological doctrine divorced from Israel is false.

Amillennialism and Postmillennialism rejects this truth.

Their appeals to 2 Timothy 2 are thereby falsified, revealed as anachronistic and hermeneutically flawed.

POINT #7
ROMANS 11, RESURRECTION,
AND THE END OF ISRAEL'S HISTORY

Most partial preterists affirm that: "The destruction of Jerusalem and the temple was the final redemptive act in the entire complex of events which inaugurated the present age" (*Mathison, 1999,* 154).[92] Sproul has stated: "No matter what view of eschatology we embrace, we must take seriously the redemptive-historical importance of Jerusalem's destruction in AD 70."[93] Boettner describes AD 70 as, "tremendously important," and "a landmark in history" (*Millennium, 1975,* 203).

One would initially think from reading the literature that partial preterists believe AD 70 was the end of God's covenant dealings with Israel. After all, that was the "break-up and abolition of the Old Testament economy" (Boettner, 1975, 203). However, many, if not most partial preterists do not believe God is through with Israel (Mathison, *1999,* 121+). Romans 11.25-27 serves as almost the sole source of authority for this idea:

"For I do not desire, brethren, that you should be ignorant of this mystery, lest you should be wise in your own opinion, that blindness in part has happened to Israel until the fullness of the Gentiles has come in. And so all Israel will be saved, as it is written: "The Deliverer will come out of Zion, And He will turn away ungodliness

---

[92] In stark contrast to Mathison's (and Sproul's) comments which emphasize the incredible spiritual significance of the fall of Jerusalem, Pratt castigates true preterists: "They reduce the nature of Christ's return to a nebulous, relatively inconsequential spiritual return in order to defend a misconceived notion of the integrity of biblical prophecy." So, on the one hand, Mathison– and we could include Gentry as well -- sees the events of AD 70 as the "final redemptive act" while Pratt says it basically meant nothing! This is just one of many, many glaring contradictions between the authors of *WSTTB*.

[93] R. C. Sproul Sr., *Last Days According to Jesus,* (Grand Rapids, Baker, 1998)26.

from Jacob; For this is My covenant with them, When I take away their sins."

We clearly do not have space to fully discuss Romans 11 here. However, we can demonstrate that it cannot be removed from its first century context. There are several things preventing a yet future fulfillment of Romans 11.

But before proceeding, we need to comment on the fact that to say there is uncertainty and confusion in the ranks of partial preterists– and commentators as a whole -- in regard to Romans 11 is a huge understatement. Among Amillennialists, as just noted above, there is the view that although Romans 11.25f uses the future tenses to speak of the coming of the Lord, that actually, Paul was speaking of Christ's Incarnate coming. Others believe the "all Israel" is to be identified as the totality of individual Jews who turn to the Lord throughout the entirety of the Christian age. Others openly express uncertainty. I could share several anecdotes in testimony of this, from my own youth, as I inquired about Romans with prominent ministers in my fellowship.

With that said, let me present some points that force us to posit the fulfillment of Romans 11 in the first century.

1. Israel's salvation would come "when the fullness of the Gentiles is come in." (11.25). However, the fullness of the Gentiles is not a numeric fullness, but the completion of bringing the Gentiles into full equality with the Jews, in Christ. This process was the distinctive and personal responsibility of the apostle Paul (Romans 15.16f; Colossians 1.24-27).[94]

2. The salvation of "all Israel" would be the consummation of the process of saving the remnant. That process was already ongoing as Paul

---

[94] See my *Who Is This Babylon* for an extensive discussion of Paul's distinctive and special role in bringing in the fullness of the Gentiles. This has tremendous implications for the proper understanding of eschatology, but is seldom applied to Romans 11.25f.

wrote (Romans 9.24f; 11.5f). Further, Paul said the salvation of the remnant would be consummated shortly (Romans 9.28).[95]

3. It is widely recognized that Romans 11.25f anticipated the fulfillment of Isaiah 27 and 59 and Jeremiah 31. What is so significant is that both Isaiah 27 and 59 posit the salvation of Israel at the time of the judgment of Old Covenant Israel for shedding the blood of the martyrs. And of course, Jesus said that all the blood of all the martyrs would be avenged in the judgment of Jerusalem in AD 70.

4. In conjunction with point #2, it must be recognized that Paul viewed the coming salvation of Israel, the climax of the salvation of the remnant, as *resurrection*:

"For I speak to you Gentiles; inasmuch as I am an apostle to the Gentiles, I magnify my ministry, if by any means I may provoke to jealousy those who are my flesh and save some of them. For if their being cast away is the reconciling of the world, what will their acceptance be but life from the dead?" (Romans 11.13-15).[96]

Holland offers this: "Paul is not saying that her (Israel's, DKP) acceptance is a future event which will happen before the resurrection of the dead. He is saying the resurrection of the Jewish people has taken place, or is taking place (1 Corinthians 15.52; cf. Hosea 13.14 [cited in 1 Cor. 15.55]; Ezekiel

---

[95] Mathison seeks to negate this argument by delineating between the remnant and "all Israel." He says the remnant was the believing of Israel, while "Israel" was the then currently hardened Israel. While this is undeniably true, it overlooks the fact that even the remnant were unbelievers *until they turned to Christ in faith*. Thus, the salvation of "all Israel" most assuredly could have been the consummation of the salvation of the remnant by the process of "the rest of the remnant" turning to Christ in faith. Even Mathison does not posit the salvation of truly "all Israel." Why go outside of Paul's definition of those being saved and violate his temporal parameters to interpret Romans 11?

[96] Note how Isaiah posits the resurrection as the time of the salvation of Israel also (25.8-9).

37.1-14; Daniel 12.2). If this is the imagery Paul is alluding to, he writes that in turning to Messiah, Israel is being resurrected from spiritual death"[97] Wright takes a similar position, commenting on Romans 11.15: "The high probability then seems to be that whenever one or more Jews become 'jealous' and turn in faith to the God who has now revealed his covenant plan and purpose in the Messiah (10.1f) that event ought to be understood by the church, particularly its gentile members, not as a peculiar or even unwelcome event, but as another bit of 'resurrection,' to be celebrated as such."[98]

From these points alone, it should be clear that in the mind of the apostle, the climax of Israel's history, in fulfillment of YHVH's promises to her, Israel would receive "life from the dead." This is *Torah to Telos*; it is corporate resurrection of the "body" of Israel, transformed into the body of Christ.

As just noted, Jesus said not one jot, not one tittle of the Old Law would pass, and that means God's relationship with Israel would not be terminated, until it was all fulfilled. In light of Romans 11.15 we could even express it in terms of resurrection: Until Israel was raised from the dead, Torah could not pass. Thus, if the Covenant promises remain valid, the sacrificial mandates that are expressions of that Covenant relationship, remain valid as well. You cannot maintain a future for Israel without at the same time asserting that Israel remains God's covenant people. Yet, the partial preterists deny Israel is still God's covenant people. This is a logical fallacy of major proportions.

5. The prophecy of Isaiah 59 foretold the salvation of Israel at the coming of the Lord in judgment of Israel for shedding innocent blood

---

[97] Tom Holland, *Romans The Divine Marriage*, (Eugene, OR., Pickwick Publications, 2011)376.

[98] N. T. Wright, *Paul and the Faithfulness of God,* (Minneapolis, Fortress, 2013, Vol. II)1200. Wright rejects the idea that Romans 11.15 referred to physical resurrection. It is the corporate salvation of Israel. Like Holland, Wright pays scant attention (virtually none) to the context of the prophetic source of Paul's prophecy.

(Isaiah 59.5-12). This motif is almost universally ignored by the commentators.[99]

None of the contributors to *WSTTB* say one word about the prophetic source or context lying behind Romans 11. There is total silence about the theme of martyr vindication in Isaiah 27 and 59. In fact, Mathison is the only contributor to even mention Romans 11 (2004, 200f). He posits a future conversion of Israel. But this, to reiterate, ignores the prophetic source of Romans 11.25f that undeniably posits the anticipated salvation in the context of the judgment of Israel for shedding innocent blood. Romans 11 plays a crucial role in our understanding of eschatology, of God's dealings with Israel and soteriology. For Mathison to wrongly apply it, in his attempts to refute Covenant Eschatology, shows his misunderstanding of Paul's eschatological narrative. For the other contributors to that work to totally ignore Romans 11 is inexcusable.

Jesus made it abundantly clear in Matthew 23 that the judgment of Israel for shedding innocent blood, "all the blood of all the righteous shed on the earth" (Matthew 23.33f), would occur in AD 70.[100] Thus, Romans 11.26f foretold the fulfillment of Isaiah 59. But Isaiah 59 is the coming of Christ in judgment of Israel for shedding innocent blood. Christ came in judgment of Israel for shedding innocent blood in AD 70. Therefore, Romans 11.26f was fulfilled at the coming of Christ in AD 70.

6. If Romans 11 has not been fulfilled, Jeremiah 31.29f has not been fulfilled and *the New Covenant has not been established.* Jeremiah 31 foretold the time when God would take away the sin of Israel by

---

[99] Although Holland takes note that Paul draws from Isaiah 59, he says not one word about the context of martyr vindication that plays such a dominant role in Isaiah's prophecy.

[100] In April of 2002, Ed Stevens and I debated two Amillennialists. I presented an affirmative on Romans 11 and the resurrection. The material visibly stunned our opponents and they literally said not one word in response.

establishing the New Covenant with them.[101] The Old Covenant could never take away sin, but the New Covenant could. But if Jeremiah has not been fulfilled, the New covenant has not been made, because it was the *New Covenant* whereby Israel's sins would be removed.[102] If the New Covenant has not been established to take away Israel's sin, that means the Old Covenant is still binding.

Notice the correlation with Daniel 9. Jeremiah 31 says God would take away Israel's sin by making the New Covenant with them. In Daniel 9 Jehovah said seventy weeks were determined to take away Israel's sin. Here is the argument simply stated:

☞ Seventy weeks were determined to take away Israel's sin (Daniel 9.24f).

☞ But, the taking away of Israel's sin would be accomplished by making a New Covenant with Israel (Jeremiah 31).

☞ Therefore, seventy weeks were determined for the making of the New Covenant of Jeremiah 31.

The making of the New Covenant, from initiation to consummation, belongs to the seventy weeks of Daniel 9. You cannot have the initiation of the New Covenant to begin within the seventy weeks and the perfection of that Covenant outside the seventy weeks. That violates the text. However

---

[101] How can God establish or even fulfill the promise of the New Covenant with "ethnic Israel" when no such entity exists today? All genealogical records verifying the identity of "ethnic Israel" perished in AD 70. Even Jewish authorities agree there is no such thing as a "race" of Israel, descended from Abraham today. See my book *Israel, 1948: Countdown to No Where*, for a fuller discussion of this.

[102] John Walvoord says if it could be proven that the New Covenant has been established, "it would be a crushing blow to the Premillennial contention that there is a future kingdom." (*Major Bible Prophecies,* Grand Rapids, Zondervan, 1991)186. The truth is, it can be demonstrated with ease that the Jeremiad Covenant has been established.

long therefore, you extrapolate the fulfillment of Romans 11 into the future, *it is that far you delay the revelatory and confirmatory process of the New Covenant.*

☞ Romans 11 anticipated the fulfillment of Jeremiah 31 and Daniel 9.

☞ But, Jeremiah 31 and Daniel 9 are confined to the seventy weeks.

☞ Therefore, the fulfillment of Romans 11 is confined to the seventy weeks of Daniel 9.

Romans 11 anticipated the taking away of Israel's sin through the promised New Covenant. That promised removal of sin is confined to the seventy weeks. This demands the parousia of Christ, to bring the New Covenant to perfection, belongs to and is confined to the seventy weeks of Daniel 9.24.

We would also take note that Gentry and most Postmillennialists argue that the charismata, *including the revelatory and confirmatory process of revelation* was completed in the first century.[103] This means the New Covenant of Jeremiah 31 has been perfected. But, if the New Covenant of Jeremiah 31 has been completed, then undeniably, *Romans 11.25f has been fulfilled!* At whatever point of time you posit the perfection of the New

---

[103] Actually, there is a good bit of confusion in the Dominionist world about the charismata. Joel McDurmon wrote an article on "That Which Is Perfect." http://americanvision.org/?s=That+Which+is+Perfect.
 In that article, McDurmon noted that he had been a member of the charismatic movement for over five years but had never witnessed a genuine miracle. Nonetheless, he equivocated about whether there are living prophets today, insisting that even if there are, reports of such would be simply unprovable and inconsequential. So, even if there are still living, inspired, authoritative, infallible prophets today, it would not matter? I wrote a lengthy series of articles responding to McDurmon's article. The first in that series is found here: http://eschatology.org/index.php?option=com_content&view=article&id=1268:joel-mcdurmon-on-1-corinthians-13-a-response-1&catid=131:uncategorised.

Covenant, it is at that juncture that you posit the completion of the seventy weeks and it is that point at which you posit the fulfillment of Romans 11.

This has tremendous implications for those who posit the fulfillment of the seventy weeks in 34-35 AD. The taking away of Israel's sin cannot be divorced from the making of the New Covenant (Jeremiah / Romans 11). The making of the New Covenant demands not just the initiation, but the *consummation* of that revelatory and confirmatory process, as Gentry argues with Gruden. However, Gentry posits the end of the seventy weeks at 34-35. This means the revelatory and confirmatory process was completed by AD 34-35, because Gentry has the end of the seventy weeks at that point. Gentry would object to this, yet, his position demands this is true. Note his position:

a. The seventy weeks of Daniel 9 were fulfilled circa AD 34-35.
b. The New Covenant of Christ was perfected in the first century.
c. The charismata, God's means of revealing and confirming the New Covenant, have ceased with the completion of that process.

Yet,

d. We are (supposedly) still awaiting the fulfillment of Romans 11, that promised the taking away of Israel's sin by the making of the New Covenant. (Now, were Gentry to argue that Romans 11 speaks of the application of the New Covenant and not the making of the New Covenant, it would demand that he abandon his argument on Daniel 9 that the making of Atonement refers to the objective reality and not the subjective application.)

Gentry's position is inherently self contradictory, because he fails to see the connection between Daniel 9, Jeremiah and Romans 11. All of these events are inextricably bound up with one another and thus, belong to the seventy weeks.

God was in the process of establishing the covenant promised in Jeremiah when Hebrews was written (Hebrews 8.6f). The Old Covenant was "old and nigh unto vanishing away" (Hebrews 8.13).[104] Since the promised New Covenant was being made and the Old was in the process of passing away, this all but demands that the "salvation of Israel" was near. It was to be the parousia of Christ that would finally sweep away that Old Law, the "ministry of death written and engraven in stones" (2 Corinthians 3.5f) and fully establish the New Covenant.

---

[104]Interestingly, millennial leaders acknowledge Jeremiah's New Covenant "would replace the Mosaic Covenant." So, Jeremiah's New Covenant would take away sin and it would replace the Mosaic Covenant. The New Covenant of Christ (The Messiah of Israel, sent to fulfill her promises), has replaced the Mosaic Covenant and takes away sin. Yet, we are supposed to reject the gospel as the fulfillment of Jeremiah and believe the New Covenant of Christ that "will never pass away" (Matthew 24.35), will one day give way to the Jeremiad Covenant that will mandate an entire list of commands that are now *forbidden* by Christ. Think about it. Christ's Covenant forbids animal sacrifice, physical circumcision, imposition of dietary laws, observance of Sabbaths, mandatory travel to Jerusalem, ethnic and racial distinctions, etc.. Yet, according to Millennialism, all of these things will be divinely mandated under the Jeremiad New Covenant. Well, if that is so, what happens to the eternal gospel of Christ that can "never pass away"? In fact, Millennialists do believe the gospel will be replaced or abrogated in the millennium. This is surely a horrid thought.

POINT #8
HYMENAEAN HERESY HYPOCRISY

Now that we have exegetically presented the issues behind 2 Timothy 2 and have proven that resurrection belonged to Israel, we want to return now to look closer at the charge of heresy being leveled against proponents of Covenant Eschatology based on 2 Timothy 2. It is our intent to show that those who are making the charge are guilty of a sort of theological hypocrisy.

Both the Amillennialists and Postmillennialists argue that God has now cast off Old Covenant Israel. Boettner says the events of AD 70 constituted, "the break-up and abolition of the Old Testament economy" (*Millennium*, 203). Israel no longer holds her exclusive place in God's scheme. Of course, Postmillennialists insist "all Israel shall be saved," but this salvation is not related to *Israel's eschaton*. It occurs "at the end of human history as we know it." In other words, according to Postmillennialists, Israel reaches her destiny at the end of the Christian age.

The Millennialists on the other hand refuse to acknowledge the temporal parameters divinely established for the fulfillment of Israel's promises. They postpone Israel's eschaton from the last days that were in existence in the first century (Acts 2; Hebrews 11; 1 Peter, etc.) and extrapolate Israel's last days into our future. This is a distortion of the inspired text and has no theological merit.[105]

The focus of the rest of this work will center not only on the charge of heresy, but, it will focus on things we have established above and how they relate to the text of 2 Timothy 2. We will show that instead of Covenant Eschatology being a resurrection of the Hymenaean Heresy as charged by Sandlin, Sproul Jr., Mathison, Gentry, etc., it is Amillennialism and Postmillennialism (especially) that must answer the charge of *why those respective views are denying the faithfulness of God*. They must answer the question of what right do they have to divorce Israel from her promises, her eschaton and her hope and create a totally new eschaton unknown in scripture. They must answer the question: if it was heretical to say the

---

[105] See my *The Last Days Identified* book for a full demonstration of the proper identity of the Last Days.

resurrection had occurred, before it did occur, what does it mean for them to not only deny it has occurred, but to say it has nothing to do with the people to whom it was promised? These are but a few of the issues to be covered in the rest of this work.

As an Amillennialist I was raised believing God was through with Israel at the Cross / Pentecost period. Beginning on Pentecost, God established the church and from that point forward God has dealt with the church exclusively. There are no future promises for Israel -- *period*! However, through intensive, long term study, I determined that this doctrine has no Biblical merit.

Consequently, in public debates with Amillennialists I have asked, "At what point of time and with what event were all of God's promises to Israel fulfilled and His covenant relationship with her terminated?" In the majority of those debates my opponents have responded, "At the Cross" or, "In AD 70."[106]

The idea that the promise of the resurrection belonged to *Old Covenant Israel after the flesh*, was and still is to many, especially to Amillennialists and Postmillennialists either unknown, ignored or denied. This truth is a

---

[106] It has been interesting to see a shift in Amillennialists in regard to this question. With the growing awareness of Covenant Eschatology, more and more Amillennialists with whom I come in contact are willing to concede that God's dealings with Israel were not terminated until AD 70.

crushing blow to the Amillennial and Postmillennial views.[107] Let me illustrate.

Prominent Postmillennialist Lorraine Boettner said this of Old Testament prophecies made to Israel: "For information concerning the first coming of Christ, we go to the Old Testament. He came exactly as predicted and all those prophecies were fulfilled or were forfeited through disobedience. But for information concerning his Second Coming and what future developments will be, we go only to the New Testament."[108] This seems to be the view of all the contributors to *WSTTB* as well.

In spite of these claims, Paul is emphatic that his doctrine of the resurrection was nothing but the hope of Israel found in the Old Covenant. *He never calls it the "hope of the church."* Yet, that is precisely what Christianity through the ages has labeled the resurrection doctrine. They have ripped the promises of Israel away from her and transferred them to the church. This is precisely what is happening when futurists go to 2 Timothy 2 and call preterists heretics.

They are ripping Israel's promises away from her. This is what was happening in Romans 11 and Paul emphatically condemned that view.

---

[107] In reality, it is also devastating to the Millennialists who see 1 Corinthians 15 as predictive of the rapture (*Tim LaHaye and Thomas Ice, Charting the End Times*, Eugene, Or. Harvest House, 2001)111. Well, the rapture is supposed to be all about the church, to put an end to the church age and not about the fulfillment of God's promises to Israel. Yet, Paul, in Corinthians 15 affirms that his resurrection doctrine was based squarely on the OT promises to Israel (v. 54-55). If therefore 1 Corinthians 15 is the rapture, that means *the rapture and the church were revealed in the OT.* If 1Corinthians15 is the rapture of the church and if 1 Corinthians 15 is from the OT, it therefore follows inexorably that the rapture and the church were foretold in the OT.

[108] Lorraine Boettner, *Four Views of the Millennium*, (Downers Grove, InterVarsity, 1977)102.

They are divorcing those promises from the climax of Israel's covenant age. They are positing fulfillment of those promises at the end of the endless Christian age.

Yet, God said His promises to Israel after the flesh were "irrevocable." While some promises found in the Tanakh were conditional and contingent, God's promise to save Israel at the end of the age and the parousia of her Messiah was irrevocable (Romans 11.25-29). It was not conditional or contingent. God's sovereignty guaranteed fulfillment– in spite of Pratt's claims.

Now, since the resurrection belongs to the end of the age and since resurrection belongs to Israel, it therefore follows that Biblical Eschatology is "Jewish" eschatology. Biblical eschatology has to do with the fulfillment of God's promises to Israel, at the end of *her* days, at her eschaton.

Fact: Resurrection belonged to Israel.
Fact: Resurrection would be at the end of the age.
Fact: Therefore, unless Israel's promises were to be fulfilled at the end of a different age from the age representing Israel and her promises, resurrection belonged to the end of Israel's Old Covenant age.
Fact: Therefore, for the New Testament writers to affirm the nearness of the end of the age—in fulfillment of Israel's promises, *was to affirm the nearness of the resurrection.*
1 Corinthians 10.

The resurrection undeniably belonged to Israel. Resurrection is linked with "the end of the age." It therefore follows, unless we want to argue that Israel's promises have failed, or been ripped from her and transferred to another people to be fulfilled at the end of another age,[109] -

---

[109] Christ was the first fruit of the resurrection of those who had died before him (1 Corinthians 15.12-21). His resurrection was definitely in the last days of Old Covenant Israel, not the last days of the church age (Galatians 4.4; Hebrews 9.26). Are we to suppose that the first fruits of the harvest occurred at the end of one age, but the harvest will not

- the resurrection was to occur at the end of the age of Old Covenant Israel.[110]

In addition, since resurrection belonged to the end of the age of Israel and since the New Testament writers say they were living in the last days of Israel foretold by the Old Testament prophets, it therefore follows that when they said the end of the age was near, they were affirming in the clearest manner possible that the resurrection was near. Thus, when Paul said, "The end of the ages has come upon us" (1 Corinthians 10.11), he was saying that everything the previous ages had anticipated and foretold, including resurrection, was now near. You cannot divorce resurrection from the Old Covenant age of Israel and the end of the age was to occur in the first century.

RESURRECTION BELONGS TO ISRAEL

If resurrection did not occur at the end of the age of Israel (AD 70), but is at the end of the church age, did God *postpone* or *divorce* his resurrection promises to Israel?

Did God *fail to fulfill* Israel's promises at the climax of Israel's age?

Will Amillennialists and Postmillennialists posit a *postponed eschatology?*

Those who attempt to use 2 Timothy 2. 8 to condemn preterists need to ask themselves several questions and these are questions that by and large, even

---

occur until the end of another age? Such a suggestion is in violation of Paul's harvest symbolism in Corinthians.

[110] Since the Bible affirms that the Christian age has no end (Matthew 24.35, Ephesians 3.20f; Hebrews 12.28f) it is *prima facie* false to speak of the resurrection occurring "at the end of the current Christian age." Yet, this is precisely what my opponents in several formal debates have affirmed. The *only* age that was to end was the Old Covenant age of Israel.

preterists are not pressing hard enough, in my opinion. Yet, unless the futurists are willing to deal forthrightly with these issues, they have *no ground whatsoever* to utilize 2 Timothy 2 as a charge against Covenant Eschatology.

The promise of the resurrection belonged to Israel "after the flesh" and was to occur at the end of Israel's age. If therefore Israel's eschaton, her last days arrived at the Cross, Pentecost, or in AD 70, as affirmed by Amillennialism and Postmillennialism, did God transfer Israel's promises to the church? How did He do that if His promises to her were *irrevocable*?

If Israel's last days came in the first century and the resurrection did not occur, *did God postpone His promises to Israel*, as the Millennialists– and now, Mathison's esteemed contributors -- claim?

Remember, Richard Pratt said: "Much as Israel's return from exile was expected soon and realized in part, the New Testament teaches that the blessings of Christ' return were expected soon and realized in part. As Israel's glorious return from exile was delayed because of a lack of repentance, Jesus' glorious second coming was delayed because of a lack of repentance" (2004, 154). Of course, it needs to be noted that Mathison, chief editor, objects strenuously to the idea of a postponed, delayed kingdom. He *stridently condemns* the Dispensational doctrine of the delay due to unbelief. And yet, he included that "false doctrine" in his book!

Did God fail to fulfill His promises to Israel at the end of Israel's age, the time He had appointed for the fulfillment of those promises? If in fact Jehovah failed to fulfill His promises when He promised to fulfill them, then in fact, He failed and is not faithful, Richard Pratt notwithstanding.

The very faithfulness of God is at issue here. For Hymenaeus to say the resurrection was past was to say Israel's last days had been climaxed by the fulfillment of God's promises to her. On the other hand, to say Israel's last days are past, but the resurrection has not occurred, is to say God has not been faithful to Israel. This is a serious charge indeed.

Those who would use 2 Timothy 2 against preterists are almost all in agreement that God's relationship with Israel was terminated in the first century and the Mosaic Law was abrogated, being replaced by the New Covenant of Christ.

The Postmillennialists try to say the Mosaic Law has been removed, yet they look to a future fulfillment of the Old Covenant promises made to Israel when "all Israel shall be saved." This violates Jesus' emphatic statements in Matthew 5.17-18.

Amillennialists insist God was through with Israel at the Cross, Pentecost, or AD 70. Yet, resurrection is supposedly still future. However, Paul said resurrection was part of "the Law," and Jesus said none of "the Law" could pass until all of it was fulfilled. The Amillennial view dichotomizes Israel's eschaton and her promises.

Likewise, the Millennialists insist the Mosaic Covenant and Law has been forever fulfilled and removed. Yet, they also say the resurrection is still future.

> **You cannot posit resurrection in the future and insist on the past termination of God's Covenant relationship with Israel without thereby inferring:**
>
> **1. The *transference* of her promises to the church. This creates a *New Eschaton*, unforeseen in scriptures.**
>
> **2. The *abrogation* of her promises. Yet, her promises were irrevocable.**
>
> **3. The *postponement* of her promises. This is a violation of God's prophetic word.**
>
> **4. The *failure* of God's promises to Israel. This is a violation of God's faithfulness.**

All three futurist views attempt to use 2 Timothy 2.17f to condemn preterists, without realizing they are themselves in violation of God's word by divorcing God's resurrection promises to Israel from the end of the Mosaic Covenant age, and the first century.

If you claim God kept all of His promises to Israel and terminated His covenant relationship with them in the first century, as some futurists do, you are thereby implying the resurrection was fulfilled in the first century. You cannot affirm fulfillment of all of God's promises to Israel, *at any point of time*, without thereby affirming fulfillment of resurrection, for resurrection was "the hope of Israel."

On the other hand, if you say, as all three futurist eschatologies do, that resurrection has not occurred, you are thereby demanding the continuing validity of the Old Law and Israel as the chosen people of God.

Those who attempt to use 2 Timothy 2 to condemn preterists are therefore, in serious violation of the word of God.

Virtually all adversaries of Covenant Eschatology who attempt to utilize 2 Timothy 2 in their attacks, believe 1 Corinthians 15, 1 Thessalonians 4, Revelation 20, etc. all predict the future resurrection. They overlook the fact that Paul preached nothing but the hope of Israel when he proclaimed the resurrection, and John's eschatology in Revelation is as surely drawn from the Old Covenant promises. Thus, when we read of the resurrection in Corinthians, Thessalonians, Revelation, *we are reading about Israel's hope.*

As we have seen, as long as God's promises to Israel were unfulfilled, Israel remained His people and the Old Law (and that includes the sacrificial system) remained valid and binding. Paul responded to those who said (prematurely) that God was already through with Israel by insisting God's promises to Israel were to be fulfilled at Christ's parousia (Romans 11.25-27). Therefore, Israel's covenant relationship with God would remain intact until the parousia.

Clearly, those who attempt to use 2 Timothy 2 against preterists have not considered the implication of their own futurist paradigm. *You cannot affirm the futurity of resurrection without affirming the continuing covenant relationship between God and Israel.*

It is also clear from the creeds and historical councils, not to mention the "tradition" of the church, that this is an area of theology in tremendous need of re-examination. This is truly an issue in which the church, although "reformed" needs to be "ever reforming," for this is an issue that has been virtually ignored throughout history.[111]

> **Since resurrection and Israel are inseparable, if the resurrection has not occurred:**
>
> **Israel remains God's chosen people.**
> **(Contra Amillennialism and Postmillennialism)**
>
> **Israel's eschaton has not come.**
> **(Contra Amillennialism and Postmillennialism).**
>
> **The Old Testament remains valid**
> **(Contra all futurists).**
>
> **The curse of the law remains!**

Patently, those who attempt to label preterists as heretics by an appeal to 2 Timothy 2, have not thought through the issue very clearly. To affirm the futurity of the resurrection demands:

1. That Israel remains God's chosen people, for He could not cast them off until He had faithfully kept His irrevocable promises to her.

2. Israel's eschaton has not arrived and yet, all three futurist eschatologies affirm, to varying degrees, that Israel and her Old Law did cease to function as God's chosen people, in the first century.

---

[111] We must at least give some credit to the millennial scheme for recognizing the centrality of Israel in God's last days schema. However, their failure to honor the first century fulfillment of that story and their suggestion of Jesus' failure and postponement of God's plan and the focus on the restoration of the Old Covenant form as opposed to the revelation of the "body of Christ" in fulfillment, are tragic.

3. If the resurrection has not occurred, the Old Law remains valid, for as we have seen, Jesus said not one single iota of the Old Law could pass until the entirety of the Law was fulfilled. Resurrection was part of "the law" that had to be fulfilled. Therefore, if the resurrection has not occurred, "the Law" remains valid.

4. If resurrection has not occurred, "the Law" remains valid and this means the curse of the Law remains valid. Paul believed resurrection was when the strength of sin, "the Law" and the sting of death, sin, would be conquered (1 Corinthians 15.54-56).

You cannot (properly) affirm the present victory over sin and the passing of "the Law" without affirming the reality of resurrection life. You cannot (properly) affirm the futurity of the resurrection without affirming the abiding presence of the curse of the Law.

Virtually everyone agrees that Romans 11.25f discusses the climax of Israel's history.[112] Needless to say, there is tremendous controversy about the proper interpretation. However, all three futurist schools, with some exceptions, place the fulfillment in the future.[113]

Here is what is certain:
1. Romans 11 deals with the consummation of *Israel's history*.[114]

---

[112] This is especially true of the Postmillennial and Premillennial views. The Amillennialists are prone to either try to "de-Israelize" the text by making it refer to the church as Israel, or by seeing it as discussion of individual Jews being converted down the stream of time. I well remember as a young minister, conferring on Romans 11 with esteemed Bible professors in the churches of Christ and being told that in all honesty, they struggled with the issues of Romans 11.

[113] Although, as we have seen, some proponents of the Reformed Amillennial view (Jordan) and Postmillennialism (DeMar, McDurmon) now see a first century fulfillment. This is truly significant.

[114] It is not uncommon for it to be claimed that "Israel" in v. 26f is in reality the church, i.e. spiritual Israel,

2. The climax of Israel's history is resurrection (Daniel 9 / 12 / 1 Corinthians 15. 54f).

3. The fulfillment of Romans 11 would be when Isaiah 27, Isaiah 59 and Jeremiah 31.29f would be fulfilled.

It follows therefore, that if Romans 11 has not been fulfilled, Israel has not reached her destiny, her promises remain valid and she remains God's chosen people.

More to the point, if Romans 11 and the parousia of Christ at the climax of Israel's history has not occurred, the Old Covenant promises to her remain unfulfilled. We find YHVH's covenant promise to Jacob– the re-affirmation of the Abrahamic covenant– in Genesis 28.15:

"Behold, I am with you and will keep you wherever you go, and will bring you back to this land; for I will not leave you until I have done what I have spoken to you."

So, YHVH promised that He would never forsake Israel, until He had fulfilled all of His promises to the Abrahamic seed. Take a quick look at the eschatological element of those Abrahamic promises.

Abraham longed for the New Creation, *the better resurrection* (Hebrews 11.13-16, 35-36). So, let me put it like this:

YHVH would never forsake Israel until He had fulfilled all of His promises to Abraham.

The promises to Abraham are identified as the heavenly country and city, the "better resurrection" (Hebrews 11.13-16, 35f).

---

bearing no relationship to Old Covenant Israel. This is untenable since the Israel in Paul's view was, at the time of his writing, *the enemy of the Cross through unbelief.* That hardly describes the church!

Therefore, YHVH would never forsake Abraham's seed, Israel, until the arrival of the heavenly country and city, the "better resurrection."[115]

This is incredibly significant. Look how this agrees with one of the grandest of the Old Covenant promises of the resurrection, in Isaiah 24-27.

For brevity, we will only give some bullet points of these chapters, known as the "little Apocalypse."

→ Isaiah 25.6-8 foretold the Messianic Banquet at the time of the resurrection. This is posited as the time of Israel's salvation (v. 9). We should also point out that this is in the context of the destruction of the city and temple (v. 1-3). In Matthew 8.11 Jesus confirmed that this resurrection Banquet was an intrinsic element of the Abrahamic hope, and, he said Abraham would sit at that banquet when "the sons of the kingdom will be cast out."

→ Isaiah 26.19-21 depicts the resurrection, but, that occurs in the context of the tribulation. Then, in v. 21 we have the coming of the Lord in vindication of the blood of the martyrs.

→ In chapter 27.9-13 we find the salvation of Israel, the taking away of her sin (which as we have seen, is Daniel 9.24f). At that time the fortified city is laid desolate, the altar turned to chalk stone, the people YHVH had created is forsaken.

So, in three separate set of verses, we find the ultimate salvation of Israel– the resurrection– posited at the time when YHVH would destroy the city, the temple and the people, bringing in a new world.

Remember, YHVH said He would not forsake Israel until He had fulfilled all His promises to Abraham.

---

[115] Note how Paul was anticipating the fulfillment of his eschatological resurrection hope at the fulfillment of Isaiah 25 and Hosea 13 – YHVH's promises to Israel, the seed of Abraham (1 Corinthians 15.54-56).

The ultimate promise to Abraham included the resurrection (Hebrews 11.35f).

In Isaiah 24-27 we find the promise of the resurrection, the time of Israel's salvation.

That promised salvation, at the resurrection, is also the time when YHVH would forget– forsake– the people He had created.

So, for emphasis, YHVH would not forsake Israel until the time when all of His promises to her were fulfilled– *the ultimate promise being the resurrection* -- and the time when YHVH *would* forsake Israel, all bound together. The consummation of Israel's covenant history and the resurrection are tied inseparably with the destruction of the city and the temple. These connections are totally ignored by the authors of *WSTTB*.

The problem here is that, as we have seen, the Amillennialists and Postmillennialists say God was through with Israel in the first century. The fortified city was destroyed, the altar was turned to chalk stones. The New Covenant is now in effect. Torah has been removed. *And yet, they deny the resurrection has occurred. They have YHVH forsaking Israel without doing the very thing He swore He would do -- fulfill all of His promises to Abraham!*

The problem here is real and it is major. The proponents of both schools appeal to 2 Timothy 2.17f to condemn the true preterists, while at the same time, they are in overt denial of God's oath to not forsake Israel until the time of the resurrection. They say YHVH has forsaken (forgotten) Old Covenant Israel, yet, according to scripture, that was not to happen until the time of the resurrection.

If Torah has been annulled and YHVH has forsaken Israel, God has fulfilled His promises to Abraham and Israel, for Jesus himself said not one jot or one tittle of the Law of Moses– *into which the Abrahamic promises had been incorporated*– would pass until it was all fulfilled. (Jesus' words are, in essence, the reiteration of Genesis 28). So, you cannot say God was through with Israel in the first century– or at any time– without thereby tacitly admitting that the resurrection promises made to Abraham and Israel have been fulfilled. *He would never forsake Israel until He had fulfilled His promises to Abraham and Israel.*

What is so sad is that while Mathison condemns preterists as Hymenaean Heretics, he is on record as affirming the fulfillment of God's Old Covenant promises to Israel!

Commenting on Hebrews 12, Mathison boldly says: "Christians are now experiencing the fulfillment of the eschatological hopes of Israel."[116] He seems to have overlooked the fact that the heart and core of Israel's eschatological hope was the *resurrection*. If one were to be consistent with these statements therefore, Mathison would be a true preterist because, from a logical perspective, if Christians are now enjoying the fulfillment of Israel's eschatological promises, *we are currently enjoying the fulfillment of the resurrection promises!* Shades of Hymenaeaus!

In another work, he said: "Under the New Covenant we *have come* to Mt. Zion. We *have come* to the heavenly Jerusalem. We *have come* to the church of the firstborn. We *have come* to Jesus, the mediator of this glorious New Covenant.... That which the Old Testament believers looked for in faith has come, and they have now received what was promised" (1999, 135-his emphasis).

What did those Old Covenant worthies long for? What was it that was promised to them, that Mathison says they have now received? It was the "better resurrection." It was the New Jerusalem; it was the heavenly country. So, once again, if one were to be consistent with these statements, they would be considered true preterists.

---

[116] Keith Mathison, *Age to Age, The Unfolding of Biblical Eschatology*, (Phillipsburg, NJ, P and R Publishing, 2009)625. Incredibly, after affirming the fulfillment of those Old Covenant eschatological promises, insisting we now enjoy that fulfillment, he then, to salvage his futurism, claims we are still waiting on those things after all: "the fullness of the blessing is yet future, because we await the consummation" (199, 135).

One has the right to ask, how it is that we have come to Mt. Zion, that Christians are now experiencing the fulfillment of the eschatological hopes of Israel, and yet then turn around and say we are still waiting for the fulfillment of those things.

If we are still waiting the final fulfillment of those OT promises– the promises to Abraham and Israel -- this means, as we have just seen, the Old Law remains fully intact and binding today. But that is not all that it means. What specifically does this mean? The next chart will explain.

If Romans 11 is not fulfilled, Isaiah 27, 59 and Jeremiah 31.29f are not fulfilled.

1. Isaiah 27 and 59 predicted the judgment of Israel for shedding innocent blood– cf. Mat. 23!! Was that not fulfilled at the end of Israel's history in AD 70?

2. Jeremiah 31 foretold *the New Covenant!!*

If therefore, resurrection has not occurred—at the end of Israel's history, Israel has not been judged *and the new covenant has not been established!*

Paul believed "all Israel" would be saved when Isaiah 27 and Isaiah 59 were fulfilled.[117] Significantly, both of these passages describe Israel's

---

[117] In 2014 I had a moderated formal Internet debate on YouTube, with Dr. Michael Brown, noted Christian apologist. I argued that Romans 11.25f would be fulfilled when Isaiah 27 / 59 would be fulfilled in the judgment of Israel for shedding innocent blood. Dr. Brown responded that this is false because Paul was discussing the *salvation* of Israel, not the judgment of Israel. When I noted that both Isaiah 27 and 59 emphatically posited Israel's salvation at the time of judgment, Dr. Brown then admitted that salvation and judgment go together. This was a significant admission. That debate is archived on YouTube at:

salvation as occurring, "when He makes the stones of the altar like chalk stones that are beaten to dust" (Isaiah 27.10f). Significantly, this time of judgment would be *the means of Israel's salvation*. In other words, Israel would be saved *by* judgment, not *from* judgment.

Likewise, in Isaiah 59, three times the prophet said the Lord was coming in judgment to judge Israel for shedding innocent blood (v. 3, 6, 7). At the coming of the Lord, the wicked would be destroyed, but the righteous would be saved (v. 17f).

We know from Jesus when Israel was to be judged for shedding innocent blood, when her altar would be totally destroyed. Jesus left no doubt about this. It was to be the judgment of Israel in AD 70. It is important to be reminded that the authors of *WSTTB* completely ignore Romans 11 in their attempts to negate Covenant Eschatology. Even Mathison's comments, as we have seen, totally miss the point. This is a huge oversight and failure on their part.

Paul anticipated the coming of the Lord at the consummation of Israel's history, when Israel would be judged for shedding innocent blood. Israel was judged for shedding innocent blood in AD 70. Therefore, Romans 11 was fulfilled in AD 70. Since the coming of Christ in Romans 11 is the consummation of Israel's history and the consummation of Israel's history is the *resurrection*, this means the resurrection occurred in AD 70.

Those who deny that the resurrection has occurred and then try to use 2 Timothy 2 against the preterist movement are implicitly denying that Israel has been judged for shedding innocent blood.

Furthermore, Paul believed the consummation of Israel's hope would be when Jeremiah 31 and the promise of the New Covenant would be fulfilled. So, since the promise of Jeremiah would be realized at the parousia (i.e. resurrection), if the resurrection has not occurred the New Covenant of Jeremiah 31 has not yet been made. The implications of this are incredible.

---

https://www.youtube.com/watch?v=H1fP1xB1gsM.

> **Romans 11: Some said God was through with Israel– her eschaton had come– Paul condemned that claim.**
>
> **2 Timothy 2.17f– Some said the resurrection (Israel's eschaton) was past. Paul condemned that claim.**
>
> **If resurrection has not come, we must affirm that God has not yet fulfilled his promises to Israel-they remain his people!**
>
> **Those who affirm the futurity of resurrection, but the completion of God's relationship with Israel, are in conflict with Paul!**

Those who utilize 2 Timothy 2 against the preterist view fail to note the similarity between Romans 11 and Timothy. In both passages the issue is the same, although few commentators seem cognizant of this. Some at Rome said God was through with Israel. This means they believed that Israel's eschaton had arrived. Her last days were terminated. Likewise in Timothy some were saying the resurrection–which is the consummation of Israel's last days hope– was past. There is a direct correlation here. To say the resurrection is past is to say Israel is no longer God's chosen because her shadow world has passed into the body of Christ, the reality.

You cannot say God is through with Israel, as all futurist eschatologies do in varying degrees, without saying the resurrection is past. You cannot say the resurrection is future without saying God is still dealing with Israel *as His covenant people*. These issues are inextricably linked. God's *promises* to Israel and God's *relationship* with Israel cannot be divorced from one another.

This is proven definitively in Romans 11.1f. Paul affirms that Israel had not been cast out. He says her promises were yet to be fulfilled, her promises were irrevocable (v. 29). The climax of Israel's history would be at the parousia (v. 26). Israel's promises and Israel's relationship with God go hand in hand. If her promises remain valid, her relationship remains valid.

Those who attempt to use 2 Timothy 2 against preterists, insist the resurrection is still future because it was future then. But by doing so, they ignore the relationship between Israel and eschatology in Scripture. They cannot claim God is through with Israel and affirm the futurity of resurrection. Strangely, however, that is precisely what all futurist eschatologies do, to varying degrees. This is the hypocrisy of the Hymenaean Heresy charge being leveled against Covenant Eschatology.

POINT #9
PAUL ON TRIAL AND THE HYMENAEAN HERESY: DIDN'T PAUL SAY HE WAS A PHARISEE– BELIEVING IN THE RESURRECTION LIKE THEY DID?

Few Bible students see a relationship between Paul's trial, 2 Timothy 2 and the Hymenaean situation. Yet, there is a direct connection. Paul was on trial for his view of the resurrection, the hope of Israel. He says this repeatedly.

Second, the Hymenaean controversy centered on the issue of the resurrection.

Remember, Paul said the hope of Israel was the resurrection. Therefore, when Hymenaeus said the resurrection was already past, this meant, without doubt, that Israel's eschaton had already arrived; her last days were past days. She had already reached her eschatological destiny; Israel's hope–Paul's gospel message -- had been fulfilled.

There is no way to divorce the Hymenaean situation from a consideration of Paul's trial therefore. If we are going to interpret scripture by scripture (*analogia scriptura*), we must consider all the evidence. Since Paul was tried for his views of resurrection and since Hymenaeus was condemned by Paul for his views on resurrection, we must examine the two situations to see if we can find any helpful evidence.

We turn then to examine Paul's trial to see what we can learn about the charge of Hymenaean Heresy.

> Paul: "I am a Pharisee, a son of a Pharisee, for the hope of the resurrection am I on trial."
>
> Pharisees: "We find no fault in this man."
>
> ### However!!!
> 7- 10 days later the Pharisees want Paul *dead* because of his resurrection doctrine! (Acts 24.13f).
>
> Why?? What is going on here?

It is amazing to read the commentators on Paul's initial appearance before the Sanhedrin in Acts 23. Because Paul said he was a Pharisee and because the Pharisees initially embraced Paul as a "good ole boy" it is assumed, even insisted, that Paul believed exactly what the Pharisees believed about resurrection.

The argument is normally framed like this:
➡ The Pharisees believed in a physical resurrection of human corpses out of the grave.
➡ Paul said he was a Pharisee and was on trial for his belief in the resurrection.
➡ Therefore, Paul must have believed in the physical resurrection of human corpses out of the grave. Charles Hill and Strimple appeal to this very argument (*WSTTB*, 2004, 99, 296).

Now, that *sounds impressive...* until one looks closer at the facts.

In Acts 23, the Pharisees said they found no fault in Paul. They believed in a future resurrection as the hope of Israel and Paul said he proclaimed the resurrection as the hope of Israel. *However*, 7-10 days later, who is it that is at Paul's trial asking for his head? It is not the *Sadducees*, because in Acts 24.13-14, Paul says his accusers believed in the resurrection. Thus, *it is the Pharisees who are now Paul's accusers and who want him dead.*

What in the world has happened in that 7-10 days? What made them go from saying, "We find no fault with this man!" to crying, "Off with his head"? We search in vain in *WSTTB* for any discussion of this significant fact. It is as if they are either unaware of that dramatic turn around, or refuse to ask, "Why did that happen?" To help us understand this dramatic turn of events, we need only to examine the life of Jesus, for in his life we find a direct parallel with Paul's.

There is no doubt the Jews desired the kingdom and there is no question that Jesus preached the imminence of the kingdom. There is no question the Pharisees initially accepted that message with a certain degree of gladness because "they believed that the kingdom was about to appear immediately" (Luke 19).

What I am suggesting is that just as the Jews longed for the kingdom and initially accepted Jesus, they then rejected Jesus when they discovered he was offering a kingdom that would not come with observation. Likewise, the Pharisees, who initially welcomed Paul's declaration of belief in the resurrection, soon discovered that Paul, like his Lord, was not offering the kind of kingdom and resurrection they desired.

At this juncture it is critical for us to briefly demonstrate that there is inseparable link between the kingdom and the resurrection. While some posit the kingdom fully arrived on Pentecost, they overlook the fact that the kingdom would come in power and glory at the time of the judgment and resurrection.

In Matthew 16.27-28 Jesus comes in glory and in judgment of all men– the resurrection. In v. 28 He comes in the kingdom. Thus, kingdom and resurrection are directly related temporally.[118]

---

[118] It is not too much to say that in Hebraic thought, loss of the kingdom, separation from the land, loss of the temple, etc. was *death*. This is how Isaiah, Hosea, Ezekiel 37 depicts it. See my upcoming book on the Sabbath for an examination of these important concepts. So, loss of kingdom = death. Restoration to YHVH was resurrection. This is the message of Ezekiel 37, Isaiah and Hosea.

In Matthew 25.31f Christ comes in the glory of the Lord. He sits on the throne (kingdom). All nations are gathered to him, the Great Assize– the time of the resurrection -- is set, and the righteous enter the kingdom. Very clearly, resurrection and kingdom are synchronous.

2 Timothy 4.1-2– Paul unequivocally posits the parousia and the judgment of the living and the dead (resurrection) at the time of the kingdom.

Revelation 11.15f – In this great text we have the time of the dead that they should be judged, and the declaration of the full establishment of the kingdom: "The kingdoms of this world have become the kingdom of our God and of His Christ" (v. 15).

The point here is that since Jesus was offering the kingdom, and Paul was preaching the resurrection (note that he likewise preached the kingdom, Acts 28.18f) they were not preaching two different things, for two different times. The time of the resurrection is the time of the kingdom. The kingdom would come in power and glory at the resurrection.

This is related to Hymenaeus. Had not Paul himself said the Colossians had been "translated out of darkness (a euphemism for death) into the kingdom" (Colossians 1.13)? Had he not likewise said the Colossians had died with Christ? Had he not said they had been buried with Christ and raised from the dead (Colossians 2.11-13)?

So, Paul and Jesus preached the same message under different terms, insofar as the gospel record and that of the epistles is concerned. But it is important to realize that their message was in fact the same, but simply under different imagery or terminology.

When Jesus preached the kingdom, he was preaching resurrection. When Paul preached the resurrection (as he preached the kingdom) he was preaching the kingdom.

When the Pharisees initially heard Jesus speak of the kingdom, they accepted him. And when the Pharisees heard Paul say he believed in the resurrection, they accepted him. But in the case of both Jesus and Paul, things quickly changed. As in the case with Jesus and the Jews, when the

Pharisees learned more about Paul's doctrine of the resurrection, they sought his life.

If Paul was preaching the resurrection the Pharisees wanted, why did they turn on him and want to kill him for preaching that resurrection? Do you fire the preacher for preaching what you want to hear? Take a look at the chart that compares the message and ministry of Jesus with that of Paul and the response of the Jews to each of them.

Jesus ➜	Jewish Response	Paul ➜	Jewish Response
Preached the promises of God to Israel	Initial enthusiasm toward the message	Preached the promises of God to Israel	"We find no fault with this man"
Preached the kingdom / resurrection		Preached the kingdom / resurrection	
Kingdom was at hand	Offered Jesus the kingdom	Kingdom had broken in	Initially accepted him
"I am the resurrection and the life"		Preached the resurrection through Jesus	
Rejected the kingdom they offered	Jews then rejected Jesus- "We have no king but caesar!"		They now seek to kill me

My kingdom is not of this world	Killed by the Jews when they realized what kind of kingdom He was offering		Pharisees sought to kill Paul for his resurrection doctrine– which they originally thought was their own.

It is clear Jesus and Paul did not preach the kind of visible, discernible kingdom and resurrection desired by the Pharisees. They proclaimed, "the kingdom (and thus resurrection, DKP) does not come with observation" (Luke 7.20f). It must be kept in mind that the kingdom and the resurrection are inextricably linked together temporally and in nature as we have just shown. So, if the arrival of the kingdom was not an observable event, it therefore follows that the resurrection would not "come with observation."

Of course, what is so interesting here is that both Amillennial and Postmillennial commentators appeal to Luke 17 in disputes with the Dispensationalists. They strongly maintain that the Millennialists need to see the spiritual nature of the kingdom and abandon the emphasis on a nationalistic, earthly kingdom.[119]

Hymenaeus proclaimed an accomplished spiritual resurrection. It is critical to state again that Paul did not correct Hymenaeus' concept of the *nature* of the resurrection and this is because Paul also proclaimed a spiritual resurrection.

---

[119] Of course, the irony here is that Dominionists then turn around and proclaim that in fact, there will yet be an earthly, physical kingdom *that will come with observation*! As noted above, McDurmon argued this in our 2012 debate. Likewise, in 2013, I debated Harold Eberle, a popular teacher in Bend, Oregon. Eberle insisted that we are still looking for the establishment of an earthly, physical kingdom. The DVDs of the Eberle exchange are available from me and the book of the McDurmon debate is as well.

Furthermore, Jesus came to be the king of Israel.

The Jews not only wanted a king to rule over them, but, they offered Jesus that throne and that crown (John 6.15).

It was not until Jesus rejected their offer of the throne and the kingdom that the Jews then turned on Jesus and rejected his offer of the kingdom as their king.

The question is, *why*? Why did Jesus reject their offer of the kingship, if He came to be king? And, if the Jews wanted a king, why did they turn on Jesus, after witnessing his awesome power to feed the multitudes and seek to kill him? You do not kill the preacher for preaching what you want, do you? You do not kill the messenger that brings tidings of victory, do you?

When the Pharisees misunderstood the *nature of the kingdom*, Jesus corrected their literalistic view: "The kingdom does not come with observation" (Luke 17.20-21); "My kingdom is not of this world."

Resurrection and kingdom are synonymous concepts and doctrines. To misunderstand the nature of one is to misunderstand the other.

Hymenaeus said the resurrection was past.

If Hymenaeus misunderstood the resurrection in the same way the Pharisees misunderstood the kingdom, why did Paul not correct that mistaken concept *just like Jesus did?*

The indisputable fact is that Paul did not correct Hymenaeus' concept of the nature of the resurrection. He corrected the *timing*!

The fact is, Jesus came to be king and establish the kingdom and the Jews wanted a king to rule over a restored kingdom. However, Jesus rejected their offer and they then rejected his offer? The burning question again is, "Why?" And the only logical answer is, they each rejected what the other was offering because what each party was offering was not what the other party wanted.

Jesus and Paul undeniably agreed in their doctrine of the end times. After all, Paul got his doctrine directly by inspiration from Jesus (Galatians 1.11f).

It is important once again to emphasize what we noted above: the time of the resurrection is the time of the kingdom (Matthew 25.31f; 2 Timothy 4.1f; Revelation 11.15f). The time of the kingdom is the time of the resurrection and the nature of the kingdom and the nature of the resurrection are the same.

With this said, note that Jesus and Paul had no disagreement with the Pharisees about when the kingdom and resurrection was to occur. They believed it was future, but near.

Second, there was no debate between Jesus, Paul and the Pharisees about the framework for the fulfillment of the kingdom and resurrection. These were to be the fulfillment of the hope of Israel.

If there was no argument over the timing or the framework of the resurrection, what does that leave? It leaves a disagreement over the *nature* of the resurrection and kingdom.

The Jews rejected Jesus because they came to understand He was not offering *the kind of kingdom* they wanted. The Pharisees rejected Paul because they came to understand the nature of the resurrection he was proclaiming. The parallel is direct! Once the Pharisees came to understand the nature of the resurrection Paul proclaimed as the hope of Israel, they turned on him and wanted his blood...precisely as they had turned on Jesus when they discovered the nature of the kingdom He was offering.

Let's turn now to take a look at how Hymenaeus fits into all this.

Jesus and Paul agreed with the Jews about the timing and the context of the promises made to Israel. They agreed that the fulfillment was future, but imminent and they agreed that the fulfillment of the kingdom and resurrection promises was to be the fulfillment of God's promises to Israel.

When we come to a comparison between Paul and Hymenaeus however, we find something different at work. There is no disagreement about the nature of fulfillment, only a disagreement about the *timing*. Paul affirmed that it was future. Hymenaeus, along with those in Romans 11 and those in Thessalonica affirmed it was fulfilled already. The only issue between Paul and Hymenaeus was *timing*. How do we know this?

Ask yourself the question we posed at the beginning of this book. If Hymenaeus and his audience believed that the resurrection was a time ending cosmic catastrophe, when every human corpse ever laid in the grave was suddenly reconstituted and raised out of the ground, how would it be possible to convince anyone that that event *had already happened*?

Furthermore, how could you convince anyone, by means of a *letter* that the literal creation burned up and time ended yesterday? Imagine receiving the mail, sitting down in your recliner and reading a letter that told you the earth no longer existed. The universe burned up yesterday. All of the grave yards are now empty. What is your response? You would patently think the sender of the letter was hopelessly deluded, or trying to play a joke on you. To believe such a letter, taken literally, would be impossible.

Well, Paul urged the Thessalonians not to be convinced by such a letter (2 Thessalonians 2.1f). It is totally impossible to believe anyone could be convinced the earth had been destroyed and all the dead raised physically. The very idea is ludicrous and impossible to conceive. Yet, if that is what the "end of the age" is to be and Hymenaeus said it was already passed, we are supposed to believe Hymenaeus was convincing people that time had already ended, earth no longer existed, there were no bodies in the graves!

How simple and *devastating* it would have been for Paul to simply write the Thessalonians and the Ephesians, or the Romans and tell them: "Hey, guys, look out your windows! What do you see? Do you see rocks and trees and birds and things? Yes? Well, okay, what does that tell you? Right! That means the resurrection and destruction of the earth has not occurred!" Argument over, point proven, slam dunk, case closed!

Yet, that was not Paul's argument, was it? Instead he told the Thessalonians some other things had to happen before the parousia and this means *the same things had to happen before the parousia of Romans and the resurrection of 2 Timothy!*

Our point here is that Paul and Hymenaeus absolutely must have agreed as to the nature of the resurrection, or else Paul would have addressed the issue of the nature, *just like Jesus did in Luke 17*: "The kingdom does not come with observation." But, should Paul not have said, "Hymenaeus, the resurrection comes with observation! Just look around, it has not happened." He patently did not say anything closely resembling this. If Jesus corrected misconceptions about the nature of the kingdom, would not Paul have done the same in the controversy with Hymenaeus? However, *the only thing Paul corrected was the issue of timing.*

Fact: 2 Timothy was written before the climax of Israel's history, the time of the resurrection (Daniel 9, 12).

It was, therefore, wrong to say the end had come before it had come (Luke 21.8).

If it was <u>heresy</u> to proclaim the end before it was accomplished...

Why is it not heresy to say Israel's age ended, without God keeping His covenant promises to her and Israel not receiving her (irrevocable!) promises?

It is time for those who attempt to use the "heresy" charge based on 2 Timothy 2 to face some serious questions. The "heresy" label is being thrown around far too often and far too lightly, with little or no thought about what Paul was saying and the issues involved in 2 Timothy.

There is no controversy among conservative Bible students that 2 Timothy was written prior to the end of the Old Covenant age of Israel that occurred with the fall of Jerusalem in AD 70.

We have shown definitively that the Bible places the resurrection, not at the end of the endless Christian age, but at the end of the age of Israel (Daniel 9, 12).

In Luke 21.8 Jesus warned against those who would come saying, *prematurely*, that the end had drawn near. This warning clearly applies to those in Thessalonica, Romans and 2 Timothy 2. Those teachers were not saying the end had drawn near, however; *they said it was over.*

So, here is the question: If it was heresy to say the end had come, before the end came, with all of the accompanying implications, why is it not heresy to say Israel's age is over, but that God did not keep His resurrection promises to her? Why is it not heresy to say God was not faithful to His "irrevocable" promises?

> **Questions for all who attempt to use 2 Timothy 2 against preterists:**
>
> **Fact: the resurrection and Israel are inseparable (Romans 8-11).**
>
> **By what authority do you separate Israel from her promises, her eschaton, her hope and give her promises to the church, at the end of the (*endless*) church age?**

There are more questions to be asked at this juncture. Those who would use 2 Timothy 2 as a ground for charging preterists with heresy need to be asked by what authority they separate Israel from her promises, her eschaton, her hope and give her promises to the church, at the end of the (*endless*) church age?

Why is it not heresy to set aside the Biblical testimony on these issues? Now, these are "thought questions" to ponder, *not accusations*. But, while they are not accusations, these questions are a challenge to anyone who wants to throw around the "heresy" charge with impunity. Those who argue that God is through with Israel, but Israel has never received her promises are, by direct implication, impugning the faithfulness of God, the inspiration of Scriptures and the mission and message of Jesus and Paul. These are serious issues indeed. And there are more questions to consider.

> **If it was "heresy" to prematurely say Israel's eschaton had arrived (Romans 11; 2 Timothy 2),** *Why is it not heresy* **to say God failed to keep his promises to Israel—no resurrection?**
>
> **Why is it not heresy to say God gave Israel's promises to the church, without fulfilling them to Israel (Romans 11.28)?**
>
> *Why is it not heresy* **to say God was unfaithful to Israel?**
>
> **Why is it not heresy to say the Old Covenant remains valid?**
>
> **You cannot affirm non-fulfillment of resurrection at the end of Israel's age without affirming postponement or failure of God's promises to Israel!**
>
> ## Is *That Orthodoxy?*

Paul called it heresy to say Israel's eschaton had arrived, before it actually arrived. Today, those who bandy around the Hymenaean Heresy charge say Israel's eschaton has come and gone, yet, *God did not fulfill His promises to her!* So, here are some more thought questions.

Why is it not heresy to say God did not keep His resurrection promises to Israel, at the end of her age?

Why is it not heresy to say God not only failed to keep His promises to Israel–even though they were irrevocable promises–but, He then took those promises from Israel and gave them to another people?

Why is it not heresy to say God was not faithful to Israel?

Why is it not heresy to say the Old Covenant remains valid and the curse of the Law is still in effect?

Is "orthodoxy" now defined as the doctrine that impugns the faithfulness of God?

Is "orthodoxy" defined as God's failure to keep His promises?

Is "orthodoxy" to be defined as God being forced to postpone His promises? Is this in fact, "orthodoxy"? If so, *it is time to reject orthodoxy and it is time to become "heretics"* i.e. it is time to be "out of step" with this kind of "orthodoxy!"

The "Orthodox" appeal to 2 Timothy 2.17f fails on all points!

It fails to honor the Israel / resurrection link.

It says God's promises to Israel:

Failed

Were postponed

Were transferred

Is *that* orthodoxy???

I submit that any appeal to 2 Timothy 2.17f as a basis for the charge of heresy against the adherents of Covenant Eschatology fails and fails *badly*, because it fails to honor the fact that the promise of the resurrection belonged to Israel after the flesh (Romans 8.23-9.3) and was to occur at the end of *her* age, not at the end of the endless Christian age.

The charge of heresy impales itself on its own sword because of its failure to honor the Biblical connection between Israel and resurrection. Furthermore, to reiterate this critical point, as we have seen, this position and charge demands that:

God's promises to Israel failed.

God's promises to Israel were postponed.

God's promises to Israel were taken from her and transferred.

Do you catch the power of this? "Orthodoxy" posits a failed God, or one that was unfaithful to His irrevocable promises, or that simply took Israel's promises away from her and gave them to another people! You will have to excuse me, but I find that kind of God, and that kind of "orthodoxy" repugnant and appalling.

Not one of these concepts can be justified from scripture. Not one of them honors God. Not one of them honors scriptural inspiration. Not one of them is true.

The question is therefore appropriate, once again, *Is this what has become orthodoxy?* Must one now dishonor God and His word to be considered orthodox by the church at large? Is this what is required to honor the Creeds, the Councils and church history?

Covenant Eschatology is the only paradigm that honors:

The Israel / resurrection bond.

The time for the resurrection –the end of Israel's age.

The Chronology of 2 Timothy 2.17f.

The Context of 2 Timothy 2.17f.

Preterism may be counter to creeds, councils, traditions and history -- it may be "unorthodox"—*but it honors scripture!!*

Sola Scriptura!!!

While fear-mongering terms like Hymenaean Heresy, un-orthodox, heterodox, false teachers, etc. are being leveled against those who espouse Covenant Eschatology and open ostracism is occurring against some, I am convinced it is time to "put the shoe on the other foot," as it were.

As we have seen, *Covenant Eschatology is the only eschatological paradigm that honors the scriptural testimony.* Covenant Eschatology is the only eschatological construct that affirms that God kept His word, as He said, when He said, *to whom He said*. All others fail to proclaim the faithfulness of God in these matters.

So, while preterism *is* counter to the Creeds, to the Councils, to church history and tradition,[120] it is faithful to God's word. *And that is all that matters.* I gladly affirm *Sola Scriptura!* So, let us now hear the conclusion of this matter.

---

[120] It is fascinating, not to mention revealing, that many of those who so stridently make the charge that preterism is counter to church tradition and the creeds have no problem taking positions that are counter to tradition and the creeds. When their own doctrines are shown to be counter to tradition and history, they very quickly turn to *Sola Scriptura*. Mathison says: "We must turn to scripture, not Augustine or Calvin, to verify the truthfulness of a doctrine." *(Dispensationalism Rightly Dividing the People of God?* (Phillipsburg, New Jersey, P & R Publishing, 995)49. Likewise, Gentry, defending his view of the early dating of Revelation and the identification of Babylon as Jerusalem (a view I heartily embrace, DKP), says: "The view that I shall present and defend below is contrary to what the vast majority of Christians believe today. Almost certainly you have been taught a radically different view at some point in your Christian journey. You may even be tempted to scoff at its very suggestion at this point. Nevertheless, I challenge you to bear with me as we wade through the evidence on this matter in Revelation. I am convinced that you will find the flood of evidence becoming a river 'that no man can cross.'" Kenneth Gentry, *The Beast of Revelation*, Revised, (Powder Springs, Ga, American Vision, 2002)18.

We have posed a virtually unanswerable question. Given the modern view of an earth-burning, cosmos-destroying, time-ending coming of a 5' 5" Jewish man out of heaven, how could Hymenaeus convince anyone that the Day of the Lord had already happened? Any appeal to 2 Timothy 2 *must* be able to answer this daunting question. I have yet to read or hear anyone offer what could be considered even a *plausible* answer to that question. I have certainly not encountered a *convincing* response.

We have interacted with what the Reformed community considers to be the definitive refutation of Covenant Eschatology. We have exposed the self contradictions, the faulty logic, the abuse of exegesis, the practice of eisegesis and abuse of proper hermeneutic. And we only touched the hem of the garment in revealing the fallacies in that book!

Our study has demonstrated *exegetically* that it is wrong to charge preterism with heresy based on 2 Timothy 2.17f.

We have shown that Paul's condemnation of Hymenaeus and Philetus is in the context of his discussion of death and life, but that his discussion has nothing– absolutely nothing– to do with biological death and life. This fact is totally ignored by those who so easily cite 2 Timothy 2 to condemn advocates of Covenant Eschatology.

We have shown that those who attempt to use 2 Timothy in this way are ignoring the historical and theological context of the passage. They are ignoring how the issue of the identity of the true Sons of God is critical to a proper understanding of what Hymenaeus was teaching. Any attempt to apply Paul's language, without a proper examination of Numbers 16 and the question of the identity of God's people, is fundamentally flawed and wrong.

We have shown that those appealing to the charge of the Hymenaean Heresy are guilty of ignoring or perverting all of the clear-cut Bible statements about the nearness of the resurrection in the first century.

We have shown that the charge of heresy based on 2 Timothy 2 ignores the inextricable link between God's resurrection promises and Israel.

We have shown that Biblical eschatology is in fact, *Covenant Eschatology* and not Historical Eschatology. The resurrection belonged to the end of Old Covenant Israel's age - *her covenant age* -- and not the end of history. Those who appeal to 2 Timothy 2 as a refutation of preterism are therefore, holding to a false framework for the end times.

We have shown therefore, that instead of falsifying Covenant Eschatology, 2 Timothy 2.17f is an indictment of the creeds, of church tradition and of modern commentators for their failure to properly exegete the Scripture. It is an indictment of all futurist views of eschatology.

While I am not actually suggesting that those who hold to the futurist view are heretics, (in contrast to how they view preterists) I most assuredly am affirming that it is time for a more in-depth look at what Paul actually said.

It is time for cooler heads to prevail.

It is time for dialogue between believers on this oft ignored issue of eschatology.

It is time for the modern church to come to grips with the daunting challenge of eschatology, as the enemies of Christ attack Him and Biblical inspiration for his supposed false predictions.

The charge of the Hymenaean Heresy leveled at true preterists is misplaced, anachronistic, hermeneutically flawed, eisegetic, illogical and unwarranted.

www.ingramcontent.com/pod-product-compliance
Lightning Source LLC
Chambersburg PA
CBHW061441040426
42450CB00007B/1155